The Bitchographies

Random Commentaries About Life, Love, and Knockoff Christian Louboutins

Written by Vivienne Vuitton

Copyright © 2021 by Vivienne Vuitton

All rights reserved. No part of this publication may be reproduced, distributed or transmitted in any form or by any means, including photocopying, recording or other electronic or mechanical methods, without the prior written permission of the publisher, except in the case of brief quotations embodied in reviews and certain other non-commercial uses permitted by copyright law.

Names of individuals have been altered to protect their privacy. Any resemblance to actual persons, living or dead, events, or locales is entirely coincidental.

Printed in the United States of America
Print ISBN: 978-1-953910-44-8
eBook ISBN: 978-1-953910-45-5

Library of Congress Control Number: 2021905292

Published by DartFrog Plus, the hybrid publishing imprint of DartFrog Books.

Publisher Information:
DartFrog Books
4697 Main Street
Manchester, VT 05255

www.DartFrogBooks.com

Join the discussion of this book on Bookclubz. Bookclubz is an online management tool for book clubs, available now for Android and iOS and via Bookclubz.com.

Thank you for having an unwavering belief in me.
Thank you for having strength for me when I didn't.
Thank you for fighting for me when I couldn't.
You are the light that eclipses the darkness, my safe habour, my reason, my never-ending possibility, and my best friend.

Love, Viv xoxo

Me Thinks I Have the Skills to Write a Quirky and Witty Ditty!

One sunny day, while sipping iced coffee with my best friend on the patio of my absolute favourite hangout—"the" coffee shop—I set down my cup and casually mentioned, "You know, I should put pen to paper and write something of epic proportion. What do you think?"

I hadn't thought the offhand statement through before the words escaped my lips. Quickly, in an attempt to justify my clumsy verbal spillage, I jokingly added, "Who knows? I might get lucky and strike it big with some esteemed publisher. Be the next Sylvia Plath and change the literary world forever."

My BFF, clearly taken aback by my bold claim, only flashed me a polite smile. It was the same patient smile an annoyed parent gives their bratty kid who won't stop babbling.

Adopting a slightly more serious tone, I took another sip from my coffee before saying, "Think about it, though; I could write a book with all my random thoughts and commentaries that normal, everyday people can relate to. Isn't it nice to know that most people are in similar situations? Isn't it great to laugh at our misfortunes from time to time?"

As I chuckled at myself, my best friend rolled his eyes and openly smirked. I could tell that he thought my spur-of-the-moment aspirations were completely delusional. Nothing more than a midlife crisis disguised by a flimsy premise for a book.

"Viv, do you have Joseph's amazing technicolor dream coat of distortion on again?"

Although I understood his doubt, for some bizarre reason, his apparent disdain ignited a spiteful flame of passion inside me.

Before he could serve me a healthy dose of the obvious, I blurted out, "Seriously, this book of mine could sell millions of copies. Then we could be living the dream."

Lifting both hands up in the universal sign of surrender, he then slowly said, "Sweetie, I know that you think you're talented, witty and funny, but can you *please* stop this insanity now? Baby doll, we are in our late thirties and forties. Okay? And I know that what I'm about to ask is going to be very difficult for you to absorb, but please, for the love of God, abandon that sinking ship of a dream now and be serious for one damn second! Please come and embrace the reality of boredom and responsibility we all have to live in. Trust me, it's not so bad once you get used to it."

Since when have I ever done vanilla and pedestrian? Ugh, no thanks…

Sensing my reluctance to acknowledge the facts, he then issued a not-so-subtle reminder. "Come on, Viv. You're no spring chicken anymore, honey."

To cement his point, he then reached over the table and plucked out one flowing strand of grey hair from my head. Like a fisherman holding up a trophy bass on the line, he dangled the strand between us—its absence of colour standing like an exclamation point before my eyes.

Never much for constructive criticism, I was immediately incensed. Within seconds, and in my typical sarcastic and unimpressed tone, I fired back, "All right, first off, Captain Obvious, why don't you tell me something that I don't already know." Stealing the dangling strand of hair back from between his pinched fingers, I threw it to the ground. "The way I look at it, these grey hairs are signs of the life experiences necessary to write a great book. The sights, the sounds, the characters—it's all up here. And besides, if you don't dream big, then your life will inevitably be filled with regrets. And who the hell wants that?"

At this, my friend simply shrugged and said, "Then please paint me a picture where—if by some crazy miracle you actually manage to market and sell this hypothetical book—we can spend summers driving about town in a shiny new Maserati or Porsche convertible. Girl, my 2012 Ford Focus doesn't even have air conditioning!"

Viewing that mischievous twinkle in his eye as his mind conjured up the image of riding around in a luxury sports car, I sunk my claws in a little deeper. "Don't you want to go shopping in NYC for Vuitton, Gabbana, Chanel and Louboutin? We always talk about it, but I think you know that talk is all it will ever amount to." With his attention now completely captivated by my empty, affluent promises, I kept the dream going so he'd properly see it. "Think about it; we could travel the globe and never spend a single moment conversing with dull and uninspiring people."

Then, in one single pessimistic moment of doubt, the bubble of endless imagination popped. All at once, the burden of reality came swooping back into the forefront of my mind.

"But then again…I *am* in my late thirties and forties with children, a career, a husband, and a mortgage. Who am I kidding? I'll never have the time or the energy to do anything great like that." Swirling the depths of my creamed coffee, the crushing realization that my dreams were mere ghosts of the past dampened my optimistic mood.

My BFF must have sensed this disappointment, and in seconds he'd flipped his previously defensive stance. "Well, when I really think about it, why *couldn't* you write a book? I mean, if it means that much to you, why not at least give it a shot, right?"

Pulled back up from both the contemplation of my drink and my self-doubt, I scanned the expression on his face for any hints of hidden sarcasm, but found none.

Maybe he's right. I'm edgy and authentic—passionate and driven. And, most importantly, I am tragically flawed. Like most unguarded souls, I have a nasty habit of wearing my heart on my sleeve. Socially awkward to the point of disability, I admit that I can be a little gullible at times. But, on the flipside, I can be a real hard-nosed bitch with a flair for the dramatic. Disconnected and complex: yup, that's me, all right.

Backpedaling away from my newfound enthusiasm, I weakly

shrugged. "I don't know. I've never written a book before. And I know absolutely nothing about the publishing world. Besides, I'm not entirely sure that anyone would even enjoy my dry, sarcastic wit." Needing encouragement like the desert needs rain, I looked my friend dead in the eye and asked, "What on earth would I even write about?"

Without missing a beat, he offered me a kind smile and casually said, "What about life? More specifically, *your* life."

After a more in-depth discussion on the concept—my overall inexperience and lack of basic writing, publishing and literary skills—I came to a final conclusion.

Meh, why the hell not? This actually might be something that I could be good at if I sit down and really put in the effort.

After decades of people-watching, of listening to my close friends talk of their great adventures and epic tragedies, I quickly concurred that I was sitting on a treasure trove of untapped material for my project. Immediately, this started a new cycle of thought including all the great topics I could cover. Fake friends, bosses from hell, idiots here, there and everywhere, and the constant nightmare of dating were just a few that drifted through my wandering mind.

You know what? I really should put all these vignettes together in the hope of maybe providing a road map for others who wish to avoid such situations. And if nothing else, maybe they'll laugh at my misfortunes and feel a little better about their own. This could be my only chance to attempt to decode the language of stupidity that so many people unknowingly engage in, to create a scholar's guide to the simpletons and moronic situations that plague our day-to-day existence in all four corners of the world.

And so, reader, here we are.

Some people may think of this book as nothing more than a self-transcribed catalogue of chronic complaints. And, in a lot of ways, they might be right. But, for my own personal taste, I'd rather refer to this collection of papers as bitchy sheets—the ones that you'd read out loud then torch in an annual burn party with the girls over a few glasses of white wine. Why not laugh and celebrate silliness? Seriously, doesn't the world already have enough problems to go around? I think so.

Anyway, back to my story.

Realizing that I had been perhaps too tense and quiet in the company of my friend, I broke from my introspective rant and flashed him a smile that waned just as quickly. Noticing my perplexed demeanor, he set down his cup and asked, "What's the matter, Viv? I thought this book thing was something you wanted to do?"

"I don't know," I sighed, my heart and mind heavy with indecision. "How the hell am I going to write a book and not draw unwanted attention? Some of the subject matter might be a little...um... sensitive."

Within seconds of posing the delicate question, we looked at each other and said, "*Nom de plume!*"

A pen name, it seemed, would protect me from any ill criticism if my book did take wings and fly around the world. But upon further thought, I suddenly acknowledged another minor conundrum, one that could ruin the whole project before it even began.

"But would a *nom de plume* lead people to believe that I am ashamed of what I'm writing? Like I'm hiding behind a mask of anonymity?"

I, of course, will never be ashamed to voice my thoughts and opinions, but I readily saw how the option of an alias could also have great benefits. Under a pseudonym, I could be more honest and open with the reader, bearing it all without fear of personal retaliation or shame. Without that shield, I could be plagued with constant questions about my work.

Who's this a reference to in chapter four, section two? Is it a close friend of yours? If so, did you base it on truth or fill in the gaps with fiction? Blah, blah, blah...

You get it. These were the pointlessly vain questions that I wished to avoid at all costs, because if by some crazy miracle my writing became popular and my name became infamous, every day would feel like the Spanish Inquisition with my family, friends and associates.

My career has led me to believe that most people, given the

opportunity, love to be the centre of attention—aka spotlight seekers—so long as the attention they receive is positive. However, this book isn't about the spotlight seekers. This is for the others who are still in a raw state. I have discovered that all people have precious egos, which can be likened to a single shard of tempered glass. This glass, though tough and sharp, is still perfectly capable of shattering into smaller pieces if put under extreme duress. The truth that my book contains has the potential to irreparably damage that fragile state for a number of people—something that I myself am not entirely comfortable with. And as much as people like to spout that they can handle the reality of their existence, very few ever really have even the slightest grasp on it. So, for their protection as well as my own, I have refrained from using anyone's real name. Instead, I decided to utilize my creativity and describe people using phrases that are reflective of their personalities.

As I've previously mentioned, I initially wanted to write a book of random commentaries and notable complaints about life, love, and my favorite shoe designer—the ultimate Christian Louboutin. But, I have been married and I have been divorced, and now I find that I have much life experience in a number of areas—one of those being dating. Unfortunately, since reentering the dating scene after my divorce was finalized four years earlier, I have been vastly disappointed by the large numbers of douchebags waiting in the wings. Oddly enough, they seem to have exclusivity on the "fresh meat" market these days.

To add to my woes, I'm also a member of the cold corporate world, where egomaniacs, calculating colleagues, insecure bosses, scheming employees, boardroom bullies, narcissists, and mindless, uninspiring idiots surround me like human barricades every single day. Don't get me wrong; I'm definitely not the girl next door, but I do have an eye for fashion and a need for luxury. But if it was within the realm of fiscal possibility, I can guarantee you that every square inch of my closet would be full of the latest Balmain, Gucci, Alexander McQueen, Stella McCartney, Chanel, and D&G collections. I suppose that I could accurately classify myself as a designer label whore with a taste for champagne, who just so happens to live on a beer budget. I'm sure you know the type.

For your reading consideration, I possess the following credentials. I am endlessly sarcastic, neurotic, cynical, and I'm a critical thinker. I engage in self-reflective practice and believe that I'm more than qualified to have a bona fide PhD in psychology from the University of Life. Even so, I must now warn you, potential reader, that the following pages are not intended for the faint of heart. There are mature themes and content to follow. So, if you're looking for Doris Day, Pollyanna, or Mary Poppins, then you should probably stop reading now. I mean, let's be honest here. I didn't entitle this book *The Niceographies*. Know what I'm saying?

With all that said, I choose to dedicate this book to all of us who struggle to bite our tongues while in the presence of idiots, senseless situations, and the other various annoyances that occupy the hairline cracks of our lives. More often than not, most of us are compliantly silent in the presence of everyday stupidity—too nice to say anything, so we simply say nothing.

So, in honour of that constant struggle, I have determined that it is high time to stop being nice. We need to tell the truth and, perhaps, share an opportunity to laugh our collective arses off! Who needs therapy when we can bitch and share war stories, right? If memory serves, didn't someone famous once say that laughter is the best medicine? In so many ways, I believe this to be true.

If you choose to continue this adventure with me, fasten your seatbelts and get ready; it's gonna be one hell of a ride!

Who Is Vivienne Vuitton?

Rather than have you read a polished, overly edited version of who I am, I would much prefer to share the "real deal" with you all. I'm currently middle-aged, and will go on record as saying that I'm deathly afraid to speak the actual number. Just like how I'm still wary of the numbers on the bathroom scale after Thanksgiving dinner, it's a brutal truth that I'd rather not think about if I can help it. As such, I've not uttered my exact age aloud to a single person since I turned twenty-one. I'm not exactly sure why I avoid this uncontrollable fact; I know that burying my head in the sand isn't going to change that dreaded number, or those that will hopefully follow. And you know what they say; the facts, my dear, are simply the facts. And that is that.

This reminds me of when my former husband asked me to marry him. We had been romantically involved for some time when, out of the blue, he popped the question one day when we met up for lunch. At the time, I was convinced that he must've been doing a little afternoon drinking. It's funny, but my first thought wasn't to consider whether or not I should say yes, but to ask myself why on earth he would want to spend the rest of his natural life with me. But, regardless of my thoughts on the idea, I did eventually say yes. And with that spontaneous marriage proposal came a never-ending barrage of mortgage and car payments, kids, and constant bickering between husband and wife. Truly, I had entered the rat race of modern living, and I found it to be less than ideal.

Yippie...

On one of my grocery shopping trips, a former acquaintance from high school approached me. We made with the typical "Hi! It's been so long," talk over zucchini in the produce section before getting into personal details. As expected, her reaction to my developments since high school was naked and brash.

"Wow!" she exclaimed once I told her that I had children and had settled down. "I'm literally dumbfounded right now! To think you settled down and had kids. Well, that's just great. I'm very happy that you're finally making the right decisions with your life."

Smiling, I looked her right in the eye and said, "Yes, indeed. Still can't believe the big guy upstairs actually granted ME the ability to reproduce. I guess he determined that the replication of my mutant DNA, while a scary concept, just wasn't scary enough to warrant divine intervention. Oh well, what can ya do?"

Uneased by my bizarre, offhand remark, she nervously looked me over one more time before scuttling away down the aisle. I haven't seen her again since.

I still can't help but wonder—was it something I said?

On a rather embarrassing note, I often secretly fantasize that I'm smokin' hot, or am at least on the fast track to total hotness. In my imagination, I'm a total bombshell—a buxom beauty who could only be rated as a ten out of ten. This delusion runs so deep, in fact, that I actively pretend talent scouts from prestigious companies like Victoria's Secret are stalking me. They want—no, NEED—me to be the next forerunner in their Angel campaign alongside Gigi or Bella and all the other flawless hotties. I am their next big star.

Except…it's all make-believe, a coping mechanism to deal with how mundane and predictable my life has become. At one point, when I was still married, my husband and I didn't even sleep in the same bed. Like modern-day Puritans, both of us had our own twin mattresses that sat on opposite sides of the bedroom. I should also add that I wore so many layers to bed that I could have easily been confused for a Sherpa leading an arctic expedition. And to be even more frank, I can't remember the last time I had sex. There, I said it. This does lead me to wonder if a person can go so long without *it* that they actually forget what to do. For my sake, I sure hope not.

"My God, woman," my then-husband used to say on those lonely nights when he practically begged me to push those two lonely beds together. "You are completely unsex-able!"

This bit of friction—or lack thereof—would always lead to more fighting and bickering, which inevitably led to talks of divorce. And so the cycle goes.

◈

Although I've been asked several times to be featured in an article of HOMES magazine, I've had to continually pass on the prestigious honour because of my...

Okay, that's never happened, but you can't blame me for trying. This is my book, after all.

Truth time: I don't live in a fancy mansion or private villa. No, my dwellings are quite humble, although an indoor swimming pool or tennis court does sound pretty nice. In *my* perfect world, I would spend each and every day shopping and acquiring brand-new shiny things—my VISA would be my best of friends. But over time, those marvelous purchases would amount to steep monthly bills with ridiculous interest rates. It is most disappointing that Louis Vuitton and Alexander McQueen insist on creating new designs and accessories every single season that I just can't live without. In my world, life without the latest Vuitton is tantamount to a long and painful existence.

To the wonderment and surprise of many who know me, I have earned various prestigious degrees and scholarships. I earnestly try to utilize the level of knowledge I've acquired in my day-to-day encounters with others. However, more often than not, my thoughts and opinions are taken out of context and get lost in muddled translation. Those who are supposedly close to me often liken me to an "educated idiot" of sorts, claiming that I lack any real common sense. Those same supposedly honest confidants have also unflatteringly described me as "book smart, but street stupid." When I'm forced to think about the summation of my life, the following description instantly comes to mind: complicated and a little bit dramatic, but not overly so. Honestly, I desperately try to be a good person with outstanding ethics and morals, but sometimes I come off as a stuck-up bitch to those who don't really know me all that well. In the past, it has occurred to me that I might be lacking a functioning verbal filter; my honesty is always blunt and precise.

Just to illustrate this point, I've decided to share with you some examples of my life that you may appreciate—for better or worse.

Well, to no surprise to all the mothers that might be reading this, raising children is undoubtedly a hard job—especially if your significant other is unsupportive or just an all-around degenerate. Once I became a mother, every fibre of my being was devoted to the welfare of my children. I have and will always make the necessary sacrifices in order to provide for them and see to it that they have a comfortable upbringing. They are my babies, after all.

Case in point: a while back, my son and I were out having breakfast with a friend of mine. The meal was perfectly fine, just a casual get-together over coffee and pancakes. On the way back to the car, with my son safely out of earshot in the backseat, my friend suddenly stopped me from getting behind the wheel and pulled me aside.

He lowered his voice, and in a flat, apathetic tone, he said, "Vivienne, there's something important I have to say…and it can't wait any longer."

At that point, I had no idea what kind of devastating news he was about to tell me. *What on earth could be going on with him? Is he sick? In debt? In trouble with the law? Oh no, I hope it's nothing too serious…*

With an expression full of truthfulness and sincerity, he gently reached out and took my hand. "We've known each other for a long time now," he said, his touch tender and openly affectionate. "And I don't want to hurt your feelings…but I've never seen you like this before. To put it simply…you look absolutely terrible. What the hell is going on with you?" He quickly added, "There's absolutely no excuse that will justify the fact that you have let yourself go to this degree."

For the first time in a long time, I was left completely speechless. Now, I ask you, what could I possibly say to that?

Without even giving me an opportunity to retort, he continued his ruthless campaign by pointing out even more of my obvious flaws. "You've gained an unacceptable amount of weight," he said, his hand still caressing mine like a consoling priest at an empty funeral. "And your hair is like a Greek tragedy. Your skin is all blemished and red, and your clothes are just as horrendous. And don't even get me started on your eyebrows; they look like two caterpillars crawled onto your face and decided to nest."

It took a lot of restraint, but I listened to all of this with unwavering patience—only able to display a crooked smile until he stopped flapping his lips. Once he finished, I nodded solemnly. At first, I couldn't bring myself to say anything. Beyond humiliated and hurt, I just wanted this nightmare of a conversation to be over with. But, brewing inside like a rumbling volcano, I could feel myself about to erupt with scorching anger. Getting more and more furious with each passing second, I internally stewed. *How dare he insult me like this! Who does he think he is?!*

As I moved away from him and attempted to get into the safety of my car, he abruptly stepped forward and held me in a loving embrace. Now stroking my hair, he tried to comfort me by whispering, "Please don't be mad at me. I'm sorry it had to be done like this, but I had to tell you the truth. It's for your own good. I just want to see you get your life back on track. I swear. Someone had to say it; that's what real friends are for."

"I appreciate your concern," I said, teeth gritted and fists clenched at my sides. "But I'm pretty sure that I have this covered."

About to lose my cool, I again broke from his hold, jumped into my car, and shut the door. In seconds, I was speeding away from him, watching his image shrink in my rearview mirror.

As I was driving home, face red and knuckles white on the wheel, my son looked up at me and asked, "Mommy, what's wrong? Did something bad happen?"

"Nothing that I won't get over, hun," I said evenly, flashing him a faint smile in the rearview mirror.

He was just a little boy, and I quickly decided that he didn't need to know the cruel and spiteful words I'd had to endure. Nevertheless, my predatory instincts told me to call this supposed "friend" of mine and explain a few things about myself. Like a high-def movie theater screen inside my own head, I could already imagine the conversation in vivid detail.

Hello? No, you better shut up and listen to me right now. I'm not sure if you're aware, but I have very little help with raising my kids. Yeah, that's right. I work my ass off to support my family on top of a plethora of other responsibilities, so you better get your facts straight! No, I don't have some sugar daddy paying my goddamn way through life!

For all the married ladies, especially those with kids, being "thin" or "ripped" is not only hard, but damn near impossible. Who has time to go to the gym for an hour when their entire day is already packed solid with chores and work? Did he even get that I have many responsibilities?

Regardless of his true motivation for the verbal attack, once I arrived home, I grabbed my phone from my purse and headed straight to the bathroom. But as I ran inside and closed the door, my phone already unlocked and ready in my hand, something caught my eye. Slowly, I turned.

Standing in front of the bathroom mirror, I gazed upon my reflection with much scrutiny. I did not like what I saw.

"Oh my goodness. Are you freaking kidding me?" I gasped, my nerves almost ready to snap like overwound piano wire.

The reflection staring back at me wasn't my own, but that of an unmanicured Cruella De Vil. I was much larger than I remembered being—"portly" wasn't even putting it nicely. Along with the streaks of grey lining my hair, my eyebrows were bushy and unkempt. It was then that I decided that it was time to get on the scale and confirm this ugly apparition. For the first time since I had my last (and final) baby, I took the risk. I already knew I wouldn't like the result, but better that I knew than the alternative.

Come on, you can do this, I encouraged myself. *You're a big girl... sorry, poor choice of words, but you know what I mean. You got this, girl.*

Taking one last deep breath to steady my shaky courage, I stepped forward and mounted the scale. Right away, my jaw dropped in utter disbelief.

I understand that pregnancy weight is hard to lose, but oh my God, I'm almost forty pounds heavier than I thought!

I suppose that my first clue should have been the fact that most of my clothes no longer fit me. At the time, I chalked it up to my faulty washer and dryer. A part of me didn't want to believe that I could ever be bigger than a size eight. The scariest part about all of this wasn't the fact that I had let myself go, but that I'd become the epitome of a human garbage disposal!

Shamefaced, I stepped off the scale and again faced the mirror to look at the pervasive lumps and wrinkles that covered my torso. Turning in a circle, I quickly realized that my ass looked like the front end of an old dump truck—ugly and flat. Somehow, my muffin top still managed to spill over the top of it all, a sight that disgusted me to my very core. Pivoting to get an even better look at my backside, I almost fell to the floor in shock at what I discovered next. Above the crest of my prominent muffin top and dump truck ass, a third flap of fat jiggled like a third breast. I had two sweater puppets in the front, where they should be, plus one spare in the back. Unable to take any more of the ghastly sight, I pulled myself away from the mirror and sat down on the hard edge of the bathtub.

In that moment of self-reflection, every instinct inside told me to weep for what I had let myself become. But instead of shedding tears of pity, I instead busted out into fits of hysterical laughter. I hate going on diets (have you ever noticed that the first three letters of the word "diet" spell the word "die"?) because invariably, I wind up feeling deprived, frustrated and sad. I knew that the only way that I could ever lose the weight was to start going to the gym, something

I never have time for. Sadly, that skinny bitch metabolism that I used to take for granted was gone. Poof, just like that—gone.

I shook my head and thought, *This is just great. Does it look like I have time to work out at the gym on top of all the other unavoidable tasks in my life?* Without much effort, the answer was a resounding NO. *For crying out loud, I'm struggling to remember to shower and brush my teeth in the morning. Now this! Why does my life have to be so complicated?*

I suddenly realized why my work colleagues were always asking me if I was feeling all right. Like a jack-o-lantern that had been left out well after Halloween to rot, they were watching me slowly implode; my once pristine form was turning into an ugly pile of gristled fat and hair.

This unavoidable truth led me to troll the internet for a quick answer to my dilemma. In my search, I stumbled upon some medical sites with images of sick people. As I scrolled through the pictures, I suddenly spied one that looked very familiar. Enlarging it, I saw that it was a full-body photo of a middle-aged woman who had suffered from the late stages of liver disease. Although she was much thinner than me, I saw the resemblance right away. My skin—which in my mid-twenties was healthy and vibrant—was jaundiced and bruised just like the woman's was in the photo. I rubbed at my pounding temples and found another fun surprise waiting for me just under my hairline. Lining the ridge of my forehead, huge, painful zits were festering just under the surface of my skin and had begun to rise.

Beyond perturbed, I bitterly asked myself, *Didn't I serve my time when I was incarcerated in hormonal prison as a teenager?! For the love of God, I don't want to spend the remainder of my thirties in a rerun of those years! This isn't fair!*

But, as I'm sure you already know, life isn't exactly fair. Is it?

Like most normal people, I often spend money on things that, if given the choice, I'd otherwise not invest in. The other day, the washing machine put in its last cycle without notice. The result of this untimely malfunction was a trip to the store for a new washer. Sounds pretty simple, right? Well...

"Why don't you just get a used machine?" my ex-husband had commented when I informed him of the dire situation. But, like always, he was way off base with his suggestion.

"First of all," I said, fixing both eyes on him like the loaded double-barrel of a twelve-gauge shotgun, "the thought of washing my clothes in a machine that some stranger soaked their dirty undies in makes my skin crawl. We are getting a new machine, and that's that."

True to my word, I bit the bullet and spent nearly $3000 on a brand-new washer and dryer. With free delivery and an extended warranty, the deal didn't seem all that bad. But still, I hated to see the money go toward something so...blah. Ya know?

Anyway, on my drive home from purchasing the washer and dryer, I quickly came to be a sobering realization. My credit card, the same one that helped me get through so many long and lonely days, had enticed me to overspend. Instead of going with perfectly fine, midrange models, I enthusiastically went with top-of-the-line products that I really didn't need. In typical Vivienne fashion, I didn't think about the *best* option, I simply chose the highest price tag. I justified this subconscious greed by reasoning, *Oh well, I have over a year to pay it off, so what the hell? Might as well go big in every way.*

And that is why, my friends, I have more debt than savings at this juncture in my life.

I'd often told myself that savings were for people planning their retirement—a rather lofty fairy tale that seemed like a million years away. Still driving along, I chuckled to myself and thought, *I honestly can't imagine when I'll be able to retire. Seriously, how does anyone ever reach that point of stability? Mind-boggling...just mind-boggling...*

Like many other women who work two jobs, I have a shift at home and a shift at the office. The two are entirely separate, but equally frustrating in their own ways. But, no matter how hard I work at either job, my former husband never failed to remind me how I was not fulfilling my wifely duties at home.

"You focus too much on work," he often grunted, recycling the same couple of sentences anytime we got into it. "I hate to say it, but you're putting your career ahead of your family. You're not cooking and cleaning as much as you should, and this is a huge problem."

Fighting the urge to smack him upside his thick head, I'd say something witty like, "Yes, I'm more than aware that neither June Cleaver nor Doris Day will be asking me to take over their positions as the queens of domesticity. Thanks for reminding me, though."

As the girl who always burns the toast, I understand I might be lacking in some wifely departments. But I still don't think it's fair that these added responsibilities were strictly mine just because—you guessed it—I was the woman of the house. God forbid he wash his own dishes or cook dinner all by himself; that'd just be asking *waaay* too much.

If reincarnation is real, I hope that in the next lifetime, I'm gifted with the blessed genitals that allow me to be this selfish and lazy without moral consequence. Maybe then I'd find some solace in life.

The following chapters are dedicated to the ties that bind, which can sometimes be full of the most unfortunate encounters and liaisons that one could imagine.

Relationships

Chapter 1
DATING R-E-D-E-F-I-N-E-D

Have you ever seen those eHarmony or Match.com commercials? Apparently, the insanely attractive guys and gals featured in the advertisements are not only beautiful, but also successful. I notice they are usually entrepreneurs or critically acclaimed professionals in their field—not to mention Nobel Prize winners and literary scholars. Seems kinda strange…but what do I know? Call it a hunch, but I have a hard time believing that any of these "single and looking" people have actually ever had challenges in dating.

After the voluntary departure from the ex, I knew that I might want to start dating again at some point. I mean, who doesn't want love and companionship? It wasn't long until I started to miss going on intimate dates to the movies and dinners out on the town. The idea of beautifying myself—curling my hair, waxing my eyebrows, applying MAC makeup (my absolute favourite), and going to the mall to buy a new outfit and shoes—was extensive, but compelling to say the least.

Truth be told, all my previous relationships could only be described as horrific disasters. Most of my close friends claim that maybe I have a sick and twisted desire to hurt myself—to subject myself to intentional misery and heartache. However, I don't think that every mishap in life must be labelled as an epic fail, and that includes failed romantic relationships. I like the concept of being with someone who would pay attention to me and laugh at my random commentaries and ridiculous dreams, all while making me feel safe and desired. I only now realize, after years and years of failed relationships with numerous Mr. Wrongs, that a man ought to defend his woman's honour and protect her pride whenever applicable. In my humble opinion, this noble attribute is of critical importance to all lasting relationships.

Unfortunately, as you get older, and you aren't fortunate enough to age as gracefully as Megan Fox or Cameron Diaz, then the issue of dating becomes increasingly complicated. There's no doubt that the challenges are significant for us all.

After my lengthy departure from the dating scene, everyone suggested I try to meet that special someone through the dreaded online dating scene! Once you plug in, you immediately take a leap of faith. There is a huge risk when you don't really know the person on the other side of the screen that hides their true thoughts and intentions. But, if you get lucky, you could find someone mildly decent among the weirdos and pervs. Not likely, but not impossible either. But then a whole new set of rules applies, which I had to learn the hard way. More often than not, I can't help but wonder if all those steak dinners were really worth the hassle in the end.

The first thing that will happen when you become single and foolishly mention your newfound status in some type of benign comment in casual conversation, everyone you know—friends, acquaintances, colleagues and strangers alike—will come out of the woodwork with their opinions. They all want the illustrious title of *matchmaker extraordinaire* and will immediately try to execute the perfect setup. Whatever you do, and please learn from my many mistakes, do not ever—EVER—entertain the idea. Trust me, not even once.

Although there will be times when you feel unbearably lonely and desperate for any kind of love, it would be best if you stayed away from the friendly hookup. Your friends will truly believe that they are being helpful and only have good intentions, but they know nothing about what's good for you. Only *you* know what's good for you—no one else. Always remember that.

A lot of the time, your friends will bring up the long list of train wreck relationships that you willingly put yourself through in the past, citing this as proof that they do in fact know better than you. To them, it's all too obvious that you desperately need help with your love life. But in the face of all this projected doubt, your mantra should remain simple. True happiness doesn't come from the outside, but from within. Intimate relationships with others are only meant to accentuate your self-derived happiness.

Nevertheless, I still find the whole dating thing to be utterly frustrating and humiliating.

These well-meaning pseudo matchmakers would approach me at work, call me at home, and pester me while shopping as well as basically anywhere and everywhere in between. They'd always act real chummy at first, inviting me out for coffee so they could present their advertising campaign for my new perfect boyfriend: BF 2.0.

When it happens to you, you scoff at the idea and decline the offer, inherently knowing that it's not meant to be. But whenever you try to interject with this valid point, you are immediately made to feel mean-spirited and pessimistic—a real wet towel.

"Oh, come on," they'll teasingly say, further trying to lower your defenses. "Don't be so negative! This guy is amazing. I'm serious! You should really reconsider." That's when they usually start playing the sympathy card and then tell you that you have a tendency to be suspicious about potentially positive experiences—a glass-half-empty kind of gal. "Not much of a risk-taker, huh?"

Foolishly, you hold back your spiteful words and politely smile. This is another serious error, as you eventually cave to their demands. Soon, another hour of your life will be wasted, never to be enjoyed again. Like sand through an hourglass…yada yada yada, you know. Of course, it's not hard for me to see that everything I was told during these romantic setups had some sort of a subversive meaning strategically attached. Before you call me crazy, please consider the following examples.

"Oh, he has a really good job," actually means, "Oh, he's rather repugnant and unattractive, but he makes a lot of money."

"He's really, really good-looking. Like, super-hot with the abs of an Olympic swimmer," directly translates to, "He's really, really stupid. Like, a super-moron with the IQ of a goldfish."

"What does he do? He's in between jobs right now. Don't worry, though, because he's stable," is pretty much, "What does he do? He lives at home with his parents. Don't worry, though, because he definitely has Star Wars bedsheets and a full-blown Peter Pan complex."

Purely out of politeness, I'd humour my friends by enduring these endless dates of sheer hell and utter boredom. I was sometimes admittedly lonely and desperate, which only added fuel to the emotionally consuming fire of my solitude.

In conclusion, here is some salient advice for all you single ladies—and fellas—out there. Avoid matchmaking schemes at all costs, because these dates are a guaranteed recipe for disaster. You're welcome.

Hear me out; I have a working theory for my group of forty-plus-year-old lady friends who have recently been through a divorce. I think they all have a subconscious need to reestablish their prior sex appeal, youth, and vitality in order to validate their own self-worth. By ensuring that some arbitrary man out at some random bar finds them attractive, they've fulfilled a primal need to attract a mate—if only for a short while. These women get the notion that this random stranger is the gold standard when it comes to determining desirability.

Now, I have no issue with anyone who parties and has a good time, but how naive can you get? I have come to the conclusion that approximately ninety percent of all men in bars are looking for one thing and one thing only: an easy lay. Seriously, that's it. They all just want a roll in the hay—or whatever you want to call it—no strings attached. Like snakes hiding in tall grass, they position themselves at the bar with the promise of free drinks and then scope the crowd for a worthy target for the night.

For example, if a man approaches you at a club and attempts to touch you in any kind of way without your prior consent, it's highly unlikely that he will be future boyfriend material. Don't get me wrong; clubs are a great place to go if you're only interested in meaningless sex. But for starting a deeper relationship, it's no good. Back in my wild twenties, I might've come to a different conclusion, but who knows? One thing's for sure, and that is that clubbing in my late thirties and forties doesn't look like much of a good time.

People will also promote the online dating avenue, swearing by its low effort and high success rate. I must admit, the option of a stress-free way of meeting people from the convenience of my computer sounded pretty nice at first. I found it a lot less intimidating than the traditional face-to-face method due to the fact that there were so many interesting profiles just waiting for me to click on. From all over the world, these potential suitors left me messages at all hours of the night. However, as I delved in deeper and began corresponding with these guys, I found that I had to spend a lot of time weeding out creeps and scuzzos from my growing list of online friends. I—with the insistence of my close girlfriends and a significant amount of research—placed a paid ad on a highly popular dating service.

This would be a good time to tell you that I have one cardinal rule in life: to abhor those who are inherently dishonest and/or stupid to a fault. When someone is that unaware, that blatantly ignorant, they tend to tragically underdeliver in every aspect of life. Because of this oath, I decided to post the truth in my ad—the way that I saw myself, not what people wanted me to be. I'm sure many of the single men who read my profile thought that the statements within were relatively harsh and uncalled for. And for that, I'm not sorry.

One guy even bothered to leave the comment, "Wow…you sound like a rude, arrogant bitch."

To which I dutifully replied, "Oh well, bypass me and move on then. I'm obviously not the girl for you."

My goal was to be as transparent as possible, and I think I accomplished just that. My ad clearly warned anyone that if they were hideous, unemployed, lived at home with their parents, viewed children as baggage, or just wanted to get laid, then I was not the woman they should pursue. I also made it very clear that I wasn't a cheap whore; I was selective and had expensive tastes. I worked hard and, therefore, thoroughly enjoyed the fruits of my labor. My children were an accessory, not a burden. And, even though my ex and I were no longer in a romantic relationship by this point, he was still the father of our children. I was never looking for a replacement in this area; to this day, I feel I fill both roles quite nicely on my own when necessary. In short, I loved my independence and was not looking for a guy who would cling to me like lint 24/7, or grow on me like a freaking fungus; I don't even like mushrooms with my steak.

But even with all this precautionary information readily available in my ad, I still ended up meeting all the wrong guys. Fun fact about me: just because a guy takes me out for a nice dinner does not mean that he's automatically entitled to jump down my pants afterward. Escort services were solely designed with that purpose in mind, buddy! I told every single one of these potential dates that I had children, but that didn't seem to curb their disgusting urges.

A part of my work position requires a significant amount of travel. So, the man I choose to date can't be insecure or possessive, either. This one guy, though, apparently didn't understand the concept when I faxed him the memo.

"I don't want you texting me or calling me every hour to see what I'm doing," I remember telling him sternly after he spent the previous night blowing up my phone. "For crying out loud, it's only ten in the morning and you've called me like a hundred times! What do you think I'm doing, nimrod? I'm at work!"

Recalling another nightmare relationship of the past, I had been talking off and on with a guy. Let's call him…Lars. Yeah, that works. Anyway, Lars seemed like a really nice guy when we initially talked on the phone. Not to mention, his profile pictures made him out to be quite the stud. Let's just say I didn't look at him and think, *Ah! I want to gouge out my eyes with a rusty spoon!*

Which, in my book, is always a plus.

After a month or so of chatting online and on the phone, we decided to meet up in person and go out on a first date. We decided on a Greek restaurant in the city, followed by a James Bond movie. I figured that a movie we would both enjoy would be a great option, and you can't go wrong with 007. During one of our lengthy conversations over the phone, I'd discovered that he, too, had travelled to Greece and enjoyed the cuisine. However, Greek restaurants in the area were greatly limited. Regardless, we set a date, promising that we'd both show up at the agreed time.

When I met Lars later that week, he was beyond cordial. Flustered, I couldn't even remember the last time a man had been thoughtful enough to greet me with a kiss on the cheek and hold the door. For once, things were starting to look up for me. Or so I thought...

Unfortunately, as the date progressed, I quickly realized how little we had in common. While I was the kind of person that wanted to own the world, he was perfectly content with just going with the flow. I knew then that the date was destined to fail, which was fairly disappointing considering how precious my free time was. About halfway through dinner, I internally wished I could be in bed watching a girly movie, eating a big bag of chips while wearing my favorite comfy pajamas. But at the same time, I didn't want to be rude or hurt Lars's feelings. He appeared to be a fairly timid guy, and I had a strong suspicion that he was actually quite sensitive underneath the masculine social front.

After dinner was done and the waiter brought the check to the table, I squeezed out a fake yawn and pretended to check my wristwatch for the time. "It's been such an exhausting week at work," I said as he slid his credit card into the leather manifold for the waiter. "I think I'll take a rain check on the movie."

His expression changed to one of genuine disappointment. He frowned and said, "Oh...okay. Do you at least want to go somewhere for a quick drink? A nightcap? Please, just one drink."

Observing his sad, hangdog expression, I eventually caved and followed him out of the restaurant to a nearby pub for a drink.

On the way, I internally lectured myself. *I'm only going to have one drink. That's it! After that, I'm heading straight home.*

But during that one drink, Lars kept telling me how beautiful I was, and his wandering hands kept finding their way to me under the table. Right away, this made me feel extremely uncomfortable. Just for the record, I'm not, nor ever have been, a touchy-feely type of girl. Needing to get out of there, I quickly finished my drink and excused myself to leave. Heart racing, I ran from the pub and out to my car down the street by the Greek place. But as I unlocked the door and got in behind the wheel, Lars snuck up from the shadows on the sidewalk. Awkwardly, he tried to lean in through the open driver's-side window for a kiss before I could drive off. In a fit of panic, I saw his blurred shape in my peripheral vision and reflexively hit the button for the power windows, rolling it up like a reverse guillotine and trapping his head there.

"Oh my God, I'm so sorry!" I apologized profusely as I rolled the window back down and released him. "I honestly didn't mean to hurt you. You just scared me, is all."

Rubbing the creased window lines on his face, he glanced frightfully over his shoulder at me as he ran back down the street.

I didn't get a kiss, but at least I got the last laugh.

I've been in several long-term relationships and have had to make numerous sacrifices because of them, not to mention mistakes that I don't want to ever make again. I can't fathom sleeping with or performing any act of oral love (the highest form of selflessness) with anyone I don't have instant chemistry with. So, with that in mind, what would be the point in continuing with this fatally flawed fairy tale?

It wasn't long before I went on another date with a guy I met online. He was athletically built and financially successful. We had spoken on numerous occasions and seemed to get along quite well on the phone. Mutually, we decided to meet at an exclusive restaurant downtown that we both liked for the amazing food and ambience. He had originally offered to pick me up at home, but I readily declined. Call me crazy, but I like to be able to come and go as I please. Always the master of my own domain, queen of the castle.

Once we greeted each other in the foyer of the restaurant, we engaged in some light small talk until we were seated at a table in the dining area.

But before the appetizers even showed up, he leaned across the table and not-so-seductively whispered, "Hey...are you a 34D or 34DD bra size?" Staring straight down the top of my V-neck shirt, he sloppily winked and added, "Don't be embarrassed, baby. I like what I see. Be honest with me; what are the chances I'll get to see the rest of that smokin' body later tonight?" Without skipping a beat, he then turned his attention to the waitress as she brought us our drinks. He flirted with her right in front of me, justifying it by rudely commenting, "You're so hot that even our lesbian waitress wants you!"

Mortified by this abhorrent behaviour, I quickly excused myself from the table. Once alone in the washroom, I tried to regain my composure before I lost all control and bitch-slapped this guy into a coma. *Seriously, who does this prick think he's talking to?! Do I look like some kind of a trophy?! A piece of meat?! Ugh, the nerve!*

I was so angry as I left the bathroom that I accidentally bumped into the waitress who brought us our drinks.

"Are you okay?" she asked as I caught myself and kept from falling.

On sure footing once again, I responded, "Yeah...physically, I'm fine. But I just discovered that my date is the biggest asshole on the face of the earth."

Clearly understanding my anguish, the waitress took one cautionary look over her shoulder before quietly saying, "You know...I have an escape route if you're interested."

Now smiling ear to ear, I quickly said, "Abso-freaking-lutely!"

However, before I followed the waitress out to the back door, I asked if she could do one last favor for me. Using my eyeliner from my purse and a blank napkin, I wrote the following message to be delivered back to my table.

While I had a blast tonight, something much more important came up that required my immediate attention. CNN—the Saturday Night edition! Thanks again!

After several more dating disasters, I finally met a guy that I thought might work out in the long run. There were numerous long-winded conversations and a couple of uneventful dates. Unlike the others, he didn't try to get physical or inappropriate with me. Things were going so well that I even decided, at some point, I might actually be willing to sleep with him. When the time was just right, of course. However, I was told right off the bat by my close friends that there are rules regarding me and my new love interest—rules that must be followed in order to ensure a prosperous relationship.

"Since when does dating come with rules?" I'd argue with them whenever the subject came up. "How old are we—fifteen? I'll call him when I want, not when the 'rules' allow it."

Of course, they would immediately counter with more of the same. "It's more than that, Viv. The rules don't stop there; they apply to sex, too."

Apparently, if you sleep with a guy on the first date, you are instantly labelled a slut in most social standings. But if you wait until the third date, then you're supposedly in the clear. They also filled me in on Facebook and Instagram etiquette, which dictates that you wait for the guy to willingly change his status to "in a relationship" before moving forward.

"Are you kidding me? You guys make it seem like we live back in the dark ages. Since when do these rules apply?"

"They have always been in place...you just never bothered to follow them." They also let me know that I might need someone to decipher texts because, apparently, I wasn't very good at that, either.

"Are you kidding me?" I retorted, still not seeing the point. "I'm the master when it comes to people-watching and interacting. Besides, those messages are private."

During one of these recurring talks, my good friend Lainey tapped me on the shoulder and flatly said, "Look, let's be real for a second. You've only ever had two serious relationships, which resulted in marriage and kids. Remember?" She then smiled and added, "You don't really have the proper experience, and that's why you don't know the rules." Hugging me to soften the blow, she whispered, "I'd hate to see you ruin a potentially good thing by not sticking to the approved script."

The one constant nugget of truth I found in these endeavours was that, much like a good pair of shoes, dating is a huge investment. If you want to keep a pair of shoes for more than one season, it's imperative that they be classics, as opposed to a fleeting fad. There are hundreds of thousands of beautiful shoes out there, so it is of the utmost importance that you take the time to try on lots of different pairs before you decide to buy that one special set. Not only should they be visually appealing, but comfortable and secure as well.

Only then will you truly get the mileage you're looking for out of them.

Please note that reader discretion is strongly advised for this chapter.

Chapter 2
DOUBLE STANDARDS

When I escaped my first long-term relationship and reentered the fabulous single life, I remember feeling like a huge weight had finally been lifted off my shoulders. There were so many avenues for me to explore; the world was my oyster. I could hang out with my friends and dance the night away without fear of receiving a third-degree tongue-lashing when I got home. That, my friends, is true freedom.

Without a doubt, I am a good girl—a woman of high moral fibre who would never engage in gluttonous one-night stands. Back then, the very thought of waking up next to a random stranger after a night of meaningless sex literally made me feel sick to my stomach. I could never forgive myself for such a vile slipup, no matter how drunk I might have been when it happened. To me, there were only a few labels more disgusting than that of a bottom-feeding hoebag.

Why would I even want to do a dirty, nasty thing like that? I'd remind myself when guys would practically jump on me and my friends at the bars, each with a complimentary drink already in hand. *I'm a quality, top-shelf babe. The best of the best, the cream of the crop. A woman of my caliber is much too pure for an unsanitary poke and run. This goes without saying, but I'm better than that. Obviously.*

This mindset got old fast. Once I dropped this Virgin Mary façade, I stopped trying to justify my crushing loneliness with moral virtue. Deep down, I desperately longed for a physical relationship. So, the new question was whether it was possible to find someone who was not only hygienic, mature and drama-free, but was also willing to hook up with no major strings attached.

The answer, coincidentally enough, eludes me to this very day.

I suppose I initially opted for a nun-like lifestyle because I was raised in a strict Catholic household, where girls were brought up to be terrified of promiscuous sex. Those naughty urges were the devil's doing, and were never to be explored if one wanted to avoid the bottomless pits of Hell after death. At least, that's what they would tell us every week at church as we sat there smiling in our best Sunday clothes. Regardless of the hooved man with the pointy horns downstairs, I managed to clock in some decent mileage on my love odometer over the years—if you catch my drift.

I think back now at the idiot buffoons I've dated and can't help but palm myself square in the face for all the dumb choices I've made. Time and time again, I willingly shacked up with the same controlling, cruel deviants that I wanted so badly to avoid in the first place. I should have afforded myself the luxury of random, passionate sex before jumping right back into another crummy relationship. I was a grown woman, liberated and free to make my own decisions despite what other people secretly thought of me. Alas, I was just too self-conscious to ever make that jump.

Men are always high-fiving and slapping each other on the back for their latest romp between the sheets. They gauge each fling using a detailed rating system, in which each guy gains more points if the girl was a barely legal virgin queen, or a feisty older babe (what you might hear referred to as a cougar or a M.I.L.F.).

If you are a woman who enjoys promiscuous sex, this rating system will never, ever apply to you. It's designed specifically for men and their patriarchal mindsets, but not for us.

In my mind, the woman that desires a good shag with no strings attached is a pleasure-seeker, a sexual adventurer. In man-terms, she is a slut, whore, or cum dumpster. There are hundreds of derogatory terms, so just take your pick. But to most, regardless of gender, this kind of woman is destined for eternal purgatory and damnation. She is considered to be a devil spawn, a home-wrecker, or a coldhearted, money-grabbing bitch (regardless of whether the man she's with actually has any money to take or not, oddly enough).

For example, let's take a woman involved in a sexual affair with a married man. Whether she knows that he's married or not, her kind is considered the worst of the worst, the scum of all scum.

Always at the front of everyone's mind, the collective observers ask themselves, "How could she ever bring herself to do such a rotten thing like that?"

The married man involved, on the other hand, is nearly forgotten in this scenario when it comes to placing blame. He has a plethora of *Get Out of Jail Free* cards just waiting to be used. Here are just a few of those cards he might have in his deck:

* *Significant amount of stress from work or home*
* *Unresolved marriage issues*
* *Midlife crisis that predisposes him to selective amnesia*

These excuses allow the *poor* married man to somehow qualify for unquestionable redemption, or even come across as a victim of circumstance. To those on the outside looking in, the whole mishap may appear to be entirely the other woman's fault.

She took advantage of a married man, they'll speculate when dinner conversation starts to wane, a stream of negative judgment based on nothing but ignorant speculation. *I bet she lured him in, knowing he was married. Wow, what a tramp! How does she live with herself?*

More often than not in these love triangles, the man just straight-up "forgets" to mention to his new girl that he's married. Just a minor oversight, I'm sure. But seriously...how the hell do you just forget about your significant other like that? A brain fart doesn't begin to explain a mental slip of that magnitude. Believe it or not, I find that excuse kind of hard to believe, considering he remembered to take off his wedding ring before the date. Dumbass.

As a grown woman with a roster of chummy guy friends, I've heard all the typical sex stories and unsavory locker-room talk that there is. More interestingly, I've also heard about their booty call strategies when they need to scratch the itch. And after a lengthy focus group session with my girlfriends, I've decided to make a list of our honest thoughts and responses for the men who have exposed us to those most unsavory of words. This is the truth they will probably never hear, but really should.

a) Listen, you're a good-looking guy with a body to die for, but I have to tell you something. The only reason that I have decided to take you home tonight is because I find you visually appealing, like a shiny new car or cell phone. Understand? So please, when we are in the throes of passion, don't you dare speak. You'll ruin it, ya know? I'm not sure if anyone has ever told you this, but your petty talk of grandeur is utterly despicable. Who do you think you're fooling with all that hot air, huh? Not me, honey. Now, I want you to make love to me. Make me feel like a goddess. Oh, and from here on out, you will do everything I say. Got it? No questions asked. And if you have a hard time following the rules—*my* rules—don't worry. I have a roll of duct tape on my bedside table with your name on it.

b) I know you think that you have the swagger of Post Malone or Travis Scott, but dude, please—PLEASE—don't tell me about all the women you've "conquered" in an attempt to impress me. I know it's difficult for you to think outside of yourself, but literally no one cares. Like, at all. Just for the record, anybody who would be impressed by a story like that is probably missing more than a few brain cells.

c) It's no secret that you're madly in love with your male apparatus, claiming it to be the very best one in all existence. However, just so you know, it is not the biggest nor best that I've seen. Not by a long shot. Can I ask you something? Ever had anyone turn to you in bed and ask, "Are you in yet?" Yeah? I thought so. I can tell that you think you're the best lay in the universe, but

honey, you ain't all that and a bag of chips. I mean, if you were going for speed over accuracy or quality, then I might agree. Sorry, baby, but I need better than a ten-second man.
d) We just met and I am so into you. Ugh, you're turning me on like crazy right now...but I must tell you something before things progress. While we are in bed...don't you dare utter that four letter word—love—or any of that cheesy, phony sentimental crap. It really kills the mood for me. Just do what I say and keep those thoughts in your empty head. 'Kay?
e) Lastly, what is up with March 14th (men's version of Valentine's Day for those women that are not aware)? Since when has there ever been a holiday where the preferred gift is an annual BJ? Don't think that those crappy drugstore chocolates or the bouquet of moldy roses guarantee mouth love—because they don't! No matter what you, your friends, or the internet might say, there is no designated holiday for such selfish acts. Shame on you for trying.

I know a lot of women have wanted to say these words out loud, but were maybe too afraid of what others may think of them once they'd launched. First off, women are allowed to have thoughts and opinions pertaining to men and sex—even if they may seem vile and inappropriate to some. The last time I checked, we were all living in the twenty-first century—the age of progress! After all, what is the main focus of everyday life but to learn to tolerate thoughts and opinions that differ from your own?

Chapter 3
EXES

No matter how old you are—how experienced or inexperienced you may be—we all have a personal story to share. But none are so painful as the stories of our exes. No matter what commitment level you two were at when things fell apart, the bond surely felt immeasurably deep, didn't it? Like he had invisible hooks plugged right into your heart, zapping electric love through every cell.

We have all weathered unwanted drama as a result of a relationship ending. Eventually, we reach the conclusion that if a decent relationship takes so much effort to grow, but bears so little fruit, then why even bother at all? At the end of the day, is it really worth the daily aggravation just to avoid another night of going to bed alone?

I say, no freaking way. To repeat the phrase that everyone uses when a friend has just severed ties with a partner, "Oh well...there are still plenty of other fish in the sea."

What they don't tell you is that most of these fish are exactly the same—from their slimy heads to their tails. I have no reason to be dishonest with you, so trust me when I say that there are some really nice guys out there. Just make sure that you don't keep chasing the same ones over and over again.

Let's use my friend Pam as an example.

Pam has admitted to tying herself up in more than a few toxic relationships based on superficial lies and deceit. These people didn't present their true, authentic selves, but instead put up projected images of what they thought she wanted them to be. Because of this false sense of honesty and trust, Pam repeated the same abusive cycle over and over again. At the inception of each relationship, she was glorified arm candy, treated as a trophy or a status symbol. But, after a few months of pampered bliss, Pam always made the same mistake. Eager to cement things, she impulsively moved in with the guy before she had a chance to even really get to know him. The first couple of weeks—known by most as the "honeymoon phase"—usually went by without incident. I think this goes without saying, but all good things must come to an end. In only a month's time, they'd be at each other's throats about this and that. Each relationship ended badly, but that never really seemed to deter Pam from repeating the cycle.

The following are some of the more unfortunate and painful memories that Pam had to endure in one of these toxic relationships. These are not even close to all of the horrors she has to tell, but she did express that there were some details that she would rather not share in order to protect her pride.

⁂

When Pam moved into one of these supposed love nests with a guy she met at a dive bar in the city, things were pure bliss—at first. But not even a week into her new arrangement, this bliss quickly went south. Seemingly overnight, her boyfriend turned into a total control freak. She was expected to be the laundry bitch, the dish bitch, the grocery bitch: really any bitch-related service. Domineering and aggressive, he'd pitch a fit and scream at her until it all got done. To quote Pam directly, "If he came home and saw a single dirty dish in the sink, oh man, watch out."

Whenever this boyfriend (maybe douchebag, prick or jerk-off would fit better) of hers got pissed off for some arbitrary reason—which could include, but was not limited to, misplacing his keys, dinner being late, laundry not being folded the right way, you name it—Pam went to the ends of the earth to try to meet all of his needs. But the ridiculous standards were damn near impossible to attain, especially by someone who already worked a full-time job. Every temper tantrum of his would come with a heavy verbal lashing. For hours on end, he would berate and belittle her, pointing out the most sensitive of her physical and personal flaws. Through this brand of mental waterboarding, he eventually coaxed Pam into believing that she deserved to be treated this poorly. If she would only try harder, then things could be peaceful again.

"Stop being ridiculous!" he'd shout during these one-sided arguments when Pam questioned why he was being so abusive, his fists balled up at his sides as if he'd strike her at any moment. "You're looking for problems that don't exist! If anyone is to blame here, it's you! Not me—you!"

It's funny, but when I mentioned to Pam that I would be writing this chapter about her personal romantic struggles, she told me, "You know, in retrospect, I really should've just worn a sign on my back that read, 'Kick Me!' At least then he would've had a legitimate reason to treat me the way he did."

Before Pam moved in with this scuzzbag, he had presented himself as a total gentleman, the spitting image of a perfectly nice and respectful guy you could bring home to your parents. At first, he was someone who would never look down on any woman.

But it didn't last long.

As soon as he started to establish dominance in the relationship, Pam's primary responsibility became funding his lifestyle—by any means necessary. Even though he had a full-time job that paid nicely, he insisted that Pam manage and pay most of his essential bills. I dare ask, what kind of adult doesn't pay their own bills? I mean, that's literally the only aspect of adulting besides drinking and sex. But no, why should *he* have to be an equal partner in the relationship? This guy just woke up one morning and thought, *Screw the idea of 50/50. I'm just gonna take the whole damn pie.* In his feeble mind, Pam should have had to pull her weight and then some. Luckily, she had a great position at her job, one that paid very well. But because of this generous income, his financial burdens were now hers to share.

As if managing his late bills and overdue credit card fees weren't hard enough, Pam was also assigned to be his personal bondsman.

Bailing him out on numerous occasions, she even paid his way out of jail after a long night of drinking and driving. He never once offered to pay her back for the costly court fees, or even apologized for the phone calls from jail at three o'clock in the morning. To be honest, I don't think the thought of accepting fault and owning up to his mistakes ever even penetrated his thick skull.

When Pam wanted to treat herself to something nice, she was told, "No way. You should know better than to be so damn selfish and try to spend all our hard-earned money on frivolous shit we don't need. Jesus, can't you think about someone other than yourself for even a second?"

Against my better judgment, I told her that paying this lousy ingrate's bills wasn't what she had signed up for. I knew it was none of my business, but I hated seeing her being treated like something less than human by this jerk. She had initially moved in with this guy for a shot at starting a solid relationship, not to become a full-time nanny to a middle-aged manbaby. Truly, Pam had been cheated.

This creep basically did whatever he wanted, whenever he wanted—moral consequences be damned. And, God forbid Pam ever kindly asked him to help out even just a little bit around the house.

In response, he would always explode with something like, "Shut up, you selfish bitch! News flash: the world doesn't revolve around you and your needs!" Or, if she ever mentioned that she would like a night at the house alone, without any of his mooch friends hanging around, he would argue, "Listen here; this is my place, not yours. If my friends wanna come here and have a couple beers, then you better treat them with nothing but respect. Understand?"

"There was never any point in arguing with him," she would later explain to me. "One way or another, he always got his way."

Invariably, Pam's whole existence centered on catering to this pig's every whim. If not, then she would have had to face his wrath and start the whole process all over again.

At one point during her long and brutal relationship with Douchebag McGee here, she was diagnosed with having an underactive thyroid.

Because of this, she had put on a little bit of weight (maybe fifteen pounds at the absolute most). Regardless of the minor poundage, he became very angry with her about this. *Very* angry.

Over dinner one night, he set down his fork, turned to her, and flatly said, "I was hoping I wouldn't have to say anything about this, but here it goes. Starting now, you are responsible for keeping up with my standards of hotness. You will diet, exercise—whatever it is you have to do to get back in shape. I will not tolerate any fatties in this house. Not for one damn second."

So, like the obedient girlfriend that she was, Pam started taking over-the-counter weight-loss medication, religiously watching what she ate, and toning up at the gym every single day. As she was slaving away at her new diet and exercise regimen, he ironically got lazier and started packing on some extra pounds himself.

After a long night of being forced to socialize with his nitwit friends when they came over for their weekly poker game, Pam's boyfriend roughly pulled her aside in the kitchen while she was grabbing the boys more beers.

"You know, Pam," he hissed, the stench of stale beer tainting his hot breath, "you're being a real stick-in-the-mud right now."

He didn't care to know what kind of person Pam really was, what her hobbies and interests might be. If he had, then he would've already known that a smart, sensitive soul like Pam's didn't need to entertain redneck trash like that.

On a slightly unrelated note, she had found various suspicious items (sex toys, Viagra tablets, and condom wrappers) in his car and around the house. When confronted with these traces of unfaithfulness, he would explode and immediately become defensive.

"How dare you question me like this?! I'm always truthful to you! This isn't fair!"

After the questions from Pam became too much, he began locking his cell phone. All night, she would see multiple text alerts flash across the screen on his side of the bed. They, along with the frequent cum stains in his dirty underwear, were obvious enough signs of infidelity. Signs, but not solid proof. So, like a love-drunk fool, Pam turned a blind eye to these signs and continued to live the lie—one day at a time.

Oddly enough, Pam's boyfriend thoroughly idolized and revered his family and friends—basically everyone in his life other than Pam. Over time, he became the overbearing noose around her neck, suffocating her ability to live freely. Controlling, demanding, paranoid, pathetic and insecure, this guy was a real dumpster fire. Pam could never have an opinion unless it aligned with his. He dreaded the concept that she might have the capability of forming an independent thought, a thing that may one day threaten his tyrannical reign over her.

In a chess master's move of subtle but fierce manipulation, he further alienated Pam from her family and friends. This dissociation from those who offered her peace of mind made Pam feel utterly useless and unappreciated, unable to see that she was being played like a pawn. In his weird game, he wanted her to believe that she couldn't live unless she was trapped under his thumb, the pressure of which might someday transform her from a lump of ugly coal into a beautiful diamond of perfect obedience. Luckily for Pam, that degraded transformation never had a chance to come to fruition.

After she escaped that hellhole of a relationship, everyone indirectly involved with the former couple tried to vilify Pam, maintaining that the breakup was solely due to her intentional wrongdoing. Not to my surprise, his version of their breakup was completely fabricated from beginning to end, a web of farfetched lies and uncharacteristic happenings. Here was a guy that had an amazing girl that would do practically anything for him, and he blew the whole deal by being a control freak and a desperately insecure cheater that needed validation from anyone and everyone but the person who truly mattered: Pam.

Although she has never told me this, I suspect that her boyfriend had significant difficulty in keeping his negative emotions in check. But whatever his ailment was, the nightmare was over for Pam, and she could finally move on.

A short time later, I was in the city for dinner and actually saw this ex-boyfriend eating at a local restaurant that I often frequented. Unable to keep from indulging myself in a little bit of small talk, I moseyed over to his table and started gabbing. Not far out of the gate, he switched gears and half-heartedly tried to explain to me why things didn't work out with Pam.

"She doesn't know what she wants, ya know? Real complicated broad, that one, always crying about this and that. I just got sick of it and cut things off. I don't need all that drama. Honestly, I'm much better without her. By the way...has she mentioned me at all?"

Politely, I tried to explain, "Look, I don't want to engage in any disparaging conversation about my good friend." But, being the social butterfly that I am, I couldn't help but share a few choice words with him before leaving his table. "First off, there's no way I'm going to let a jackass like you get away with disrespecting Pam's honour like that. She's the one that deserves better, not you." Before he could force a response out despite his slack-jawed expression, I smiled and went on. "Wow, I really can't believe all the bullshit that you put her through for four years. She told me everything, you know. It must have been so easy for you to sit back and watch Pam work like a dog all day at a thankless job, only to come home and make your supper, clean your house, pay all the bills, cosign loans, and put up with all your childish escapades. Has anyone ever told that you have the likability of an infected toenail? Here's an idea; why don't you crawl back into your cave of miserable existence and never speak ill of Pam in front of me again. *Comprende*?"

And that, ladies and gentlemen, was the last time I saw Pam's ex-boyfriend.

Chapter 4
THE OTHER WOMAN

I constantly hear nasty stories about married men who throw away a perfectly good thing just to satisfy their physical desires for a night. Lots of women will swear on a stack of King James Bibles that their husbands, partners or boyfriends would never even consider cheating on them. Not in a million years.

"Oh, he wouldn't cheat on me," they might say, rolling their eyes at the very suggestion of promiscuity from their one true love. "We have such a great bond, like two peas in a pod. Don't worry, we tell each other everything. There are no secrets between us, trust me."

My first question to those who dare utter these foolish words or any variations thereof is, "Are you really that naive?"

Despite what anyone might try to tell you, you can't assume someone else's hidden intentions, no matter who you are in that person's life. If there are secrets, then there are secrets—nothing you can do about that. I've come to the conclusion that you'd be better off not to try and discover those secrets, no matter how damning they may be. Instead, just love, honour and respect each other. If you can do that, then things will work out...probably...

Or, perhaps you are in one of those lackluster relationships and you don't really care whether your man of the moment sticks around or not. I suspect you are looking for any excuse to terminate all ties with this guy and just need a little justification before you snip the line. If it were me, and I was in a relationship that had an exclusivity clause or sexual contract of some kind, I would expect that the person that I was with to at least be honest about his doings. If he's too busy hanging around other people, then obviously he doesn't want to be around me. Why go on living a lie just to protect each other's vulnerable sensibilities? Lay it all out there and deal with it, I say.

What's the worst that could happen?

❧

One of my good friends, Meaghan, and her common law partner had been together for seven years. During this time, they had raised two beautiful little girls together. And while Meaghan was with Peter, he always had plenty of female acquaintances.

"What can I say?" he often joked. "The ladies love me."

Regardless of this unsettling fact, Meaghan trusted Peter to be honest and true. After seven years together, why wouldn't she? There was no reason for her to think anything fishy was going on. Then, it happened.

"Oh my God, Viv! I need to tell you something!" Meaghan gasped as she caught up with me at a café. Practically yanking me out of line as soon as I got my cup, we sat down at a small table in the back. "So, Peter was going on and on about this new girl that just started at work. He was quick to mention that she was married. I'm telling you, Peter was so geared up while telling me about this girl that he was practically drooling." Apparently, Peter had told her that the new girl—Cindy—and Meaghan looked so much alike that it was uncanny. "Peter kept going on and on about how he couldn't wait for me to meet this Cindy."

This overzealous statement rightfully confused Meaghan, which led her to confide in me with her lingering suspicions.

Naturally, I, too, thought this enthusiasm was very odd. "That is pretty freaky. What did you say back, Meaghan?"

"I asked him why I would want to meet some new girl from his work, to which he never really gave me an answer. But I could tell by the look in his eye that he was up to something. Something he wasn't entirely sure if he should tell me…"

As her story goes, Peter wouldn't take no for an answer and insisted that the three of them have dinner that very night. Meaghan was annoyed by her husband's unshakable insistence, but decided not to make a big fuss about a dinner date and went along with it. Little did she know what she'd actually signed up for.

Taking pride in her appearance, Meaghan usually goes to great lengths to maintain her beauty. We had been brought up to admire and appreciate all the great fashion houses. A couple of our ultimate fashion icons were and always will be Jackie Kennedy-Onassis and Grace Kelly. We both loved and adored these women because they knew how to wow the world with their classic, timeless looks. That's why when Meaghan shared with me that Peter had asked her that night if he could "review" what she would be wearing for the evening, I flashed her a puzzled look.

My reply to this—completely rhetorical, of course—was, "You must be kidding me, right? Why would he ask you something like that?"

To my horror, it wasn't a joke, and Meaghan was just as shocked as I was. "I have no idea," she whispered. "Not once in our seven years of marriage has Peter ever taken an interest in my fashion sense or clothes. He's stylish enough, but he's certainly no Marc Jacobs or Patricia Fields when it comes to coordinating ensembles."

Meaghan went on to tell me that she had decided to wear the staple of her entire wardrobe: a classic and conservative cocktail dress that would be appropriate for almost any occasion. Apparently without hesitation, Peter told her that dress was not going to work. He then made his way to her closet and pulled out a very sexy and somewhat revealing red dress.

"I told him that I didn't think this was an appropriate look for the evening; it was a little risqué and seemed too racy to wear for a seven o'clock dinner at a steakhouse with a total stranger. But he insisted."

In full drama queen mode, he started sulking and stomping his feet about the bedroom like an angry toddler. Deciding that she didn't want to deal with this crybaby crap for the entire night, she reluctantly hung her little black dress in the closet and put on the red one. Once again, she felt a sense of unease at the oddness of the situation. Her gut and intuition were putting her on high alert, but it was too late to turn back.

When Meaghan met Cindy, Cindy moved right in for a hug and a playful tap on the ass. Meaghan is the type who doesn't like her friends invading her personal space like that, let alone a total stranger. Even in her close social circles, it's unacceptable for a stranger to encroach like that. But the disrespect didn't stop there. Cindy then turned away from Meaghan to openly flirt with Peter—giving him a few too many kisses on the cheek.

But before Meaghan could bat an eye, the three were ushered off to their table.

As Cindy played with the olive in her martini glass, she eyed Meaghan for some time before leaning over to where Peter sat and whispering, "Oh yeah, she definitely passes the test." Turning her attention to Meaghan, she then said, "It's okay if you're uneducated on the matters at hand; I will spend the night teaching you things that you thought were only possible in your wildest fantasies." With one hand drifting from her lap, Cindy placed a key card in front of Meaghan and winked. "This is the extra card for my hotel suite tonight. Hope to see you there."

"And the first thing I thought was, 'What on earth is this bitch thinking?'" Meaghan continued to rant as I sipped lightly at my steaming cup of coffee. "First of all, I got two little girls to look after, and a man that's supposed to know better than to try to mix me up in shit like this."

"What did you do?" I asked, nearly sliding off the edge of my seat in anticipation.

"I slid the card back to her, looked that chick straight in the face, and asked her who put her up to this. Cindy's response was to laugh like a bimbo as she looked uneasily from me to Peter, who sat quietly by and observed our unfolding conversation with great intrigue." Outwardly annoyed and embarrassed by the gross setup she had found herself in, Meaghan continued, "I looked at her and I said, 'Cindy, I don't know you, and after this evening, if I never have to see you again it will be all too soon. I don't think you know who you are dealing with, but I will clue you in. I am not interested in being in a lesbian tryst with you because A, I like men, and B, even if I was bi-curious, you would not be my type. I'm expensive and you, my dear, are nothing more than a cheap whore!'"

After that, Meaghan informed a still silent Peter that she needed to be taken home immediately. Quickly, he ushered her outside and, for the first time in a long time, did as he was told.

But that didn't last for very long.

"Peter suddenly started to have a meltdown right there in front of the restaurant," Meaghan went on. "I was so pissed at how entitled he was acting that I could barely stand to look at him. Then he started screaming and yelling and making a scene in front of everyone. It was so embarrassing. At that point, I was completely fed up with him and his antics."

Peter then told Meaghan that she needed to stop acting like a little spoiled, uptight bitch, or else. Meaghan was so pissed; regardless of what this idiot said to her, she was leaving. She told Peter that she needed the keys to her car.

"So, what happened next?" I asked.

Meaghan lifted her eyes and told me, "I'm pretty sure that you know how the story ends."

They were done. However, Peter had tried to explain that this relationship with Cindy wasn't sexual. Meaghan looked at him in disbelief and asked if he thought that she needed a brain transplant. As suddenly as a bolt of lightning striking, she realized that she just didn't care what his pathetic excuses or lies were anymore. She was done with him. She was done with him because he was a liar and he was disrespectful. He betrayed her; how could she ever forgive him for that?

As Meaghan drove away from the restaurant, she opened the glove compartment to look for an Kleenex, and there in plain sight was a bottle of Viagra. I asked her what she did, and she told me that she probably should have started crying, but instead started to laugh uncontrollably. When Meaghan got home that evening, she started to pack her and the girls' stuff—there was no way that she was going to stay in a relationship with a lying cheat.

It's unfortunate to think that Peter felt he could justify his behaviour by stating that he wasn't cheating. In reality, all he was doing was coveting what Meaghan wouldn't give him.

Chapter 5
THE DEVIL INCARNATE: THE MOTHER-IN-LAW

For every woman across the globe, there is one person above all others that has a greater influence on your partner's life than you do: the MOTHER-IN-LAW, or MIL. Unfortunately, she and your significant other are a package deal, and she is nonnegotiable in every facet of modern society. There's no other choice but to shut up and mind your p's and q's while around her. If you don't, that wretched woman will do anything to see your relationship crumble.

But not all MILs are vindictive hellions that want to consume your happiness and good intentions. Some are fortunate enough to have one who is supportive and just generally pleasant to be around, far detached from the stereotypical old bitch that hovers over her son like a storm cloud. For the rest of us, family get-togethers are pure torture. Like a Ginsu knife, the MIL cuts clean through your polite sensibilities with finely honed disparaging remarks and negative criticisms about anything and everything. My friend Nina has a MIL who acts warm and kind most of the time, but sneaks in little jabs when no one but her is around to witness it.

"Oh, hun, I'm sure she doesn't mean anything by it." Nina's husband Jerry passively shrugs any time she brings up his mother's candidly vindictive ways. "She's just a little old lady. You probably just misheard what she said, is all. Nothing to worry about."

But to Nina, her MIL is one mean, manipulative old coot who hates her daughter-in-law more than life itself.

Like most MILs, Nina's is an attention whore and always has to be the centre of attention whenever Jerry is around. Faking a fall or complaining incessantly about her arthritis always does the trick.

In no time, he'll be rubbing her bunion-crusted feet and actually smiling about it. Ever seen anything grosser than a forty-something-year-old momma's boy? Ew, just...gross.

But that's nothing compared to if you have children. Of course, being two hundred years old, the MIL knows absolutely everything there is about raising kids. Lucky for you, she won't hesitate to remind you of this. It's irrelevant that her frame of reference is based in the age of lead paint on pacifiers and Flintstones chewable morphine. MILs are always right, and don't you dare even think of trying to prove them otherwise. The fact that medical research and civilized society as a whole has exponentially progressed since her child-rearing years doesn't mean a thing. To anyone who brings up this fact, she automatically counters with the ol' life experience routine. I guess living into your twilight years qualifies you to be the authority on every subject, regardless of how much you actually know. When in the vicinity of a MIL, you must understand one cardinal rule that applies in every situation; if she speaks to you, just smile, nod, and pray that she gets bored and moves on to someone else soon.

But I digress—back to Nina.

Like most couples, Nina and Jerry have had their ups and downs. Nothing too unusual, just typical arguments and disagreements that plague all long-term relationships. But because Jerry was a mommy's boy, he immediately goes running to his mommy anytime he and his wife fight. Surprisingly, he doesn't seem to realize that this might actually cause further upset in his marriage.

Even so, the MIL should try to help if her adult offspring comes looking for advice. She should give it to them with an unbiased view, remembering that multiple lives could be affected by her unsavory comments. Unfortunately, Nina's MIL isn't capable of such humility. Never failing to express her opinions, no matter how ill-advised they might be, Nina's MIL relishes in watching the squabbling couple squirm and flop around for a breath of fresh air. She's so inherently evil, Nina's MIL has told her son to ditch Nina and move out.

"You don't need her," she's said, playful hate twitching in the crusted corners of her wrinkled lips. "Just do yourself a favor and dump Nina. Trust me, son, you can do much, much better than her."

Keep in mind that this woman makes these comments despite the fact that these people are raising small children together.

After these secret councils, Jerry comes home with a borrowed tune to whistle. Taking on the acidic tone of his heartless mother, he lectures Nina and says things like, "You don't know what's good for me, Nina. I deserve better than this. And if you don't start picking up the slack...well..."

This undermining behaviour plays into my theory that all MILs are attention whores and home-wreckers of a different sort. For example, when Nina got engaged, she made sure to tell her husband-to-be that she didn't want any type of showers or stag parties.

"It feels too desperate begging family and friends for money and gifts," she reasoned with him. "Just feels...weird."

Nina's philosophy on life was simple, and the thought of fundraising for her wedding seemed greedy. That left the choice of either scaling back the opulence of the services, or waiting and saving up a little more money in order to have a stylishly lavish reception. Nina made it abundantly clear to everyone involved in the wedding that the event would be modest—a fact that no one openly had a problem with. Nina's only request was that there would be no big surprises. That was it.

Nina incorrectly thought that after she had announced these simple terms that nothing could possibly go wrong. However, I'm sure you know by now that was all just wishful thinking.

About two weeks before the wedding, she was busy at work and planning to write exams for her CPA (chartered professional accountant) designation, when Jerry called her office.

"Guess what? I've got a surprise for you later."

Just to be absolutely clear, Nina hates surprises. Surprises make Nina overly anxious, a fact that Jerry was more than aware of and often teased her about.

Before she could ask what he meant, Jerry chuckled and said, "I need you to go over to my mom's place after work. I'm not supposed to tell you...but she planned a wedding shower for you."

Needless to say, Nina was furious. "Are you kidding? Please tell me you're kidding right now, Jerry. This has to be a joke. She knows I specifically asked for no surprises!"

"I know, I know," he countered, feigning an unconvincing tone of sympathy. "But you know my mom. She's just trying to do what she thinks is best. Who knows? Maybe you'll have a good time."

Stunned by how little Jerry cared about the situation, Nina took a deep breath and did her best to patiently explain the circumstances from her side. "I don't think I can go. I've got so much to do over here right now that I'll probably have to stay late."

But Jerry still didn't seem to get it. "Well, if that's the case, then you need to call my mom and tell her why you can't make it. She went through the trouble to put all this together; the least you can do is give her a courtesy phone call."

So angry that she thought she might scream, Nina wanted to hang up on him and throw the phone out of the nearest window, but didn't. Instead, she sighed and said, "All right...I'll call her later."

Once she got home that evening, she gave her MIL-to-be a call. From the first icy hello, Nina could feel the old bag's hostility radiating from the other end of the line.

"Sorry I couldn't make it today," Nina apologetically said when the silence became too much to bear. "I've been extremely busy at work and just don't have time for a shower. I appreciate that you were thinking of me, but I'm going to have to pass—"

Before she could finish, a hard *click* ended the call. In a fit of rage, Jerry's mother had hung up.

Nina wasn't at all pleased when this disrespectful behaviour continued after the birth of her daughter. A mother should be happy when one of her children gets married, and then enthralled when that marriage leads to grandbabies. But instead of sharing that joy, Nina's MIL would say awful things like, "Lookin' kinda fat, Nina. Better lose some weight fast before Jerry loses interest in you and finds somebody else."

I find this statement especially amusing coming from a woman who looks like a beached whale in slip-on shoes, but most women get overly hormonal and sensitive during and after childbirth. Hearing these unnecessary put-downs only further exacerbated it for Nina. This got even worse when Jerry's mom decided to up and move herself in without asking.

"I'll only be staying over for about a month or so," she had said offhandedly when she showed up at Nina's door with all her things. "Family is family, after all. I'd do the same for you, dear."

Ensuring that Jerry's mom was comfortable during her forced stay, a still-mending Nina slept on the couch in the living room and oversaw her newborn daughter's cradle. Jerry didn't see a problem with any of this because, and I quote, "Mom's got a bad back and can't sleep on the sofa. You don't mind, right?"

Nina's MIL never gave away that she knew how much she actually inconvenienced them, but that was probably due to the fact that she never allowed anyone to speak. She singlehandedly caused many arguments and unwanted drama in Nina's household, a sad fact that continues to this day.

Throughout the agonizing years together, Nina's MIL has made a concerted effort to sabotage every aspect of joy in her life. Like a tyrant, she stomps around the house at all hours of the day and passes judgment. And although she's getting up there in age, she still manages to manipulate Jerry and twist his malleable ego to better suit her needs.

For Nina, the nightmare has only just begun.

※

When I was a little girl, my parents taught me an extremely valuable lesson. If you can't say anything nice, then don't say anything at all.

In other words, if and when your MIL starts to try and tear you

down, just remember these three tips.
   Smile.
   Nod.
   Bite your bottom lip and don't say a word, no matter how much you really want to.

Chapter 6
GET A CLUE; I CLEARLY DON'T LIKE YOU.

For some people, there is one moment in time that is more important than all the rest. That moment is when you know that you've finally met your better half—your soulmate.

I can't explain when that moment might have happened for me, but I'm sure it must have at some point. It might have been during one of our marathon conversations on the phone, or maybe on one of those coffee dates at our favourite hangout. Maybe it was when I spilled Bolognese sauce all over my brand-new dress, or that time we did the grocery shopping together and both agreed on what we wanted for supper at the exact same time.

Whatever it may be, there is a precise moment at the crucial juncture of a special relationship in which you are both comfortable enough with one another to understand where you stand in each other's lives. Excited to introduce this person to all the other important people in your life, you take a leap of faith based on that hidden feeling of fulfillment. You want everyone to know about this person who makes you smile for absolutely no reason at all. To say it's anything other than love is an understatement.

"I know my parents will love you just as much as I do," your boyfriend will say, echoing the same exact sentiments going through your head. "I've had some pretty rough relationships in the past, but that's all behind us now." Smiling, he adds, "My friends are amazing. I love them like family, and soon you will, too. I promise."

However, the "friends" that your boyfriend describes and the ones that you later meet are NOT one and the same. These "friends" are not nearly as supportive as they pretend to be in your presence. Perhaps displeased that they can no longer bro-down like they had before—smoking, drinking, and being all-around pigs—they come to secretly hate you for splitting up their once solidified group. It doesn't take long for you to realize that you are the complete opposite of them and their respective partners. Then, you start to question whether your boyfriend can even see how sloppy and dumb his friends are.

Maybe I am the one who is missing something here? I feel so awkward knowing that I'll never be in cahoots with these people. They're just so...bleh.

You know how much they mean to him, but you still can't stand to be around any of these half-witted idiots. Truly, you are faced with a perplexing dilemma that has no real answer.

I know what you're thinking. You're stunned that these people are so important to him, even though they obviously don't add any value to his life. Like me, you're independent, sophisticated, free-spirited and expensive. I don't have some desperate need to "fit in" or be accepted because I am quite happy with my own sense of self. I am secure in who I am; I possess a strong sense of purpose and self-actualization. Because of this, I have a really hard time relating to these kinds of friends. I just don't understand why they like the things they like.

I've never asked any boyfriend to choose between me and his friends. Not once. Why would I do such a thing? They were friends long before he ever laid eyes on me, so why should I put him in such a dicey predicament? But I often felt disjointed around them and knew that I would never socialize with these people in a million years if it wasn't for my boyfriend. What the hell was I even supposed to say to them? More often than not, I later found out that these supposed "friends" were judgmental backstabbers who refused to take responsibility for what *they* said, confirming my prior suspicions.

One thing that I abhor is people who lie. Seriously, it makes me sick. In my perfect version of the world, telling the truth is a law. Any and all lies, no matter how small or insignificant, are severely penalized to the highest degree.

For example, one of my boyfriends had a longtime friend whose girlfriend (her name escapes me at the moment) was a compulsive liar, hypocrite, and gossip queen. Listening to her talk was the auditory equivalent of jamming two rusty icepicks into your ears and giving 'em a good twist. Her nonsensical, inane comments made me want to crawl out of my own skin.

Does it honestly look like I'm interested in you or your boring-ass stories? Trust me, girl, I'm not! I'd rather get a root canal and a colostomy on the same day than be put through this kind of mental torture. That's what talking to you feels like—torture! Seriously, random-girlfriend-whose-name-I-can't-remember, please just shut up and go stand in the corner. For the love of God, please, someone make it stop!

Don't get me wrong; I loved my boyfriend, but listening to his bullshit friends was going to give me a brain hemorrhage. But I didn't ever want him to feel as if he had to choose between them and me, so I started inventing creative excuses in an attempt to avoid being subjected to them, or them to me.

One day, out of the blue, they all decided as a group that they were going to punish my guy by excommunicating him. All at once, they stopped texting, emailing and calling him. Their demands were simple: us, or her (me). I'm not sure if they ever realized that they weren't punishing or hurting me by doing this, only their friend. To be honest, I was ecstatic when I found out that I no longer had to endure those idiots and their moronic shenanigans. But contrary to popular belief, I can experience empathy. Therefore, I felt bad for my boyfriend. He loved those people like they were his family, and I know it tore him up inside that they would treat him like that over something so silly.

As time passed, those same friends decided to attack me online, manufacturing crazy gossip. I suppose that confronting me in person was too much of a challenge for them. At the time, I said nothing about the lies I saw posted online, keeping my fierce wit caged up inside my head like a circus lion.

I don't need to start a petty battle of words with them, I told myself when the temptation to type something back was almost too strong to ignore. We *live in a society where everyone, no matter how stupid and ridiculous their thoughts are, is entitled to their own opinions.*

I was brought up not to waste my time giving merit to any inconsequential issues that are unworthy of my time and energy. Unlike those trolls and haters, I choose to put on my trademark Christian Louboutin shoes and take the high road—classy to the end.

Chapter 7
DUMP THAT LOSER—THEY ARE JUST A WASTE OF SKIN.

Have you ever surveyed the multitude of friends and relatives in your inner circle and found yourself wondering, "What the hell were they thinking hooking up with someone like *that*?" Well, I have explored these tirelessly, predictably doomed relationships to great lengths for many, many years. And through this diligent study work, I've come to a solid conclusion that I think would withstand even the harshest analysis from expert sociologists. Honestly, I think some people are just too good-natured to be out in the rugged lands of the dating scene. Seriously, it's like the Wild West out there, and everyone is only able to truly count on themselves for solace.

But regardless of how obvious this might be to you and me, there's always some naive soul who takes the risk and just puts themselves out there anyway. Like a timid lamb walking among the hungry wolves, they pray that only kind, trusting individuals come along and show interest. And, oh boy, will they soon be disappointed by the harsh reality.

A couple of not-so-great dates later, they meet someone who is slightly more tolerable than the others. This rando isn't perfect by any means, but that's okay. The lamb is still hopeful, still painfully optimistic. Nudged forward by an underlying fear of dying alone, they go on a few more dates before things start to get really serious, really fast. Within months, they end up getting married.

That, right there, is the exact moment when everything changes forever.

The lamb soon finds their significant other transforming into a tyrannical psychopath who mentally tortures them every single day without a shred of remorse. Lately, I've been experiencing minor whiplash from shaking my head in constant disbelief that all these kind, decent, unassuming people willingly put themselves through hell over a short-term fling turned into a full-fledged hostage situation. It's just so unfortunate—unfortunate, but entirely avoidable.

Speaking on the subject, I have a good friend who is truly one of the nicest, most generous men that I have ever met—a genuine archetype for any woman's mental image of Mr. Wonderful. So wonderful, in fact, that if I were ever single again—God willing—I would totally sacrifice our friendship and pursue a little romantic fling. Not to mention, he's got a pretty nice...

Um, on the other hand, I'll keep that one to myself.

Anyway, this friend, Bob, is currently in a relationship with a lazy, overbearing, rude bitch that treats him with little to no respect at all. She is controlling, demeaning, and just downright unpleasant to be around: a real rotten egg. Instead of calling her the first fitting C-word that comes to mind, I'll instead go with Carol.

To the best of my knowledge, Carol believes that since she allows Bob to sleep intimately with her, she is therefore fully entitled to treat him like human garbage. Under her iron rule, Bob can't really do anything aside from take a piss without having to ask her for permission first. Whether he's just going out to see a few close friends and share a beer with them, or driving to work, it all needs to be cleared by Carol first. That poor bastard has to be available to her at all hours of the day, lest he face the swift wrath of Carol. When he first told me about this craziness—all the while acting as if Carol's demeanor wasn't that strange—I thought, *Oh, Bob...you have no idea what you've stepped in...*

And Carol was not exactly shy about voicing her twisted methods of psychological control in public. "Bob does whatever I say," she once bragged after a few too many cocktails while we were out for the night with friends. "His ass exclusively belongs to me. He knows it, too." Completely dismissing Bob as he stood awkwardly at her side, she took another long sip before continuing, "I got him wrapped around my little finger, ya know? Anything I want, and this good little boy will make it happen...or else..."

Interestingly enough, Carol sandwiches these cruel statements between profound proclamations of their undying love. In the same showy, domineering vein, she hangs off his shoulders and talks way too loudly about how they are soul mates who were clearly brought together by the forces of the universe…or some such bullshit.

Cough, my ass, *cough*.

After hearing this rambling speech on heavy rotation at a dinner party one long night, I had to eventually excuse myself from the table to keep from jamming my knife and fork right through her windpipe. It thoroughly disgusted me to see someone acting in such a brash, classless fashion. Where in the world is this jackassery considered normal behaviour? Easy answer: nowhere.

But even more than all of that, I felt bad for Bob. I could walk away and ignore that loudmouthed bitch, but, like it or not, poor ol' Bob was in it for the long haul. After moving a good distance away (to the bar) and taking a much-needed breather, I ventured back over to the crowded dinner table and strapped in for round two.

"It's funny," Carol blathered on, "but if I don't feel like cleaning the house, Bob here is more than happy to pick up the slack. He lives to see me comfy and happy. Isn't that right, honey?" Without even looking across the table at Bob, I could sense his quiet reproach. But Carol just took another sloppy drink from her wine glass and added, "A good man always supports his woman, no matter what! That's what real men do. I'm a princess, and Bob is, like, my court servant or something. I don't know. Oh, you guys know what I'm trying to say, though!"

In that moment of extreme annoyance, I wanted to stand up from my chair and ask Carol if her obliviousness was intentional, or if this was the neurological side effect of eating too much lead paint chips as a child. It shames me that I have to say this, but a huge part of being an adult is taking responsibility for your own actions—that, and making a conscious effort to be a contributing member of society. But, even though this is common knowledge, here sat Carol and her big, stupid mouth: an ugly exception to the most obvious of rules.

Fed up with her salty conversation killing the mood at the dinner table, I politely interrupted Carol and said, "Excuse me, but I don't think anyone really loves getting out of bed, sitting in rush hour traffic, and spending each and every day at a job they hate. So, if you don't mind, could you please give someone else a chance to talk? Thank you."

And just like that, civility and order were brought back to the table. For the rest of the dinner, Carol drunkenly sulked at Bob's side while the rest of the table talked freely and enjoyed the friendly atmosphere.

Bob's smile—small but present—was nice to see again.

Later that same week, I managed to catch up with Bob at a local park. It was a nice rural spot with plenty of walking paths and benches, one that we often met up at during our lunch breaks. Thankfully, he was without Carol's company—a beautifully rare sight to behold, indeed.

Joining me on a steel bench that faced the small pond full of wandering birds, Bob offhandedly gushed, "Carol is just so great. I truly adore her, cherish her. I dare say she might be the one, Viv. What do you think?"

Keeping my smile wide in an attempt to cover my true thoughts, I took a deep breath and replied, "Go with your heart, Bob. Go with your heart."

I know, I know, you're disappointed in me for not being forthright with my friend. But you have to understand that, as much as I hate Carol and how poorly she treats Bob, their love life is nobody's business but their own.

Not quite satisfied with my answer, Bob pushed for more. "Well, what do you think of Carol? You like her...right? Please, be honest."

Keeping my eyes trained on the shimmering waters of the sunny pond just down the hillside, I again cut through the thick fog of my real thoughts and spared him the awful sting of truth. "I think Carol's...interesting." Sensing further questions arising, I immediately added, "All that matters is that you think Carol is great."

Sadly, Bob did think Carol was great. And for that blinding lust, he would pay dearly for years and years.

An interesting fact that most people won't readily believe is that most relationships are inherently dysfunctional from the get-go. Granted, not all, but most. For those of you who have never had your bare feet put to the searing flames of broken love, please consider the following scenario.

There's a happily married couple—young, bright, and full of promise for a prosperous future together. But, after the first two years of bliss flutter by, a problem arises. You see, the husband is caught multiple times getting a little too friendly with some of the single ladies at his workplace. The wife probes the husband about his vile actions, to which he innocently claims that his roving hands and filthy mind were caused by a fundamental lack of sex at home. Like a stray cat prowling the neighborhood alleyways for its next free meal, he took anything and everything that came his way. Now found out, he profusely apologizes for his lapse in judgment and begs his wife for forgiveness.

But instead of giving her husband a break and choosing to move on, she decides to take another approach. Shifting into an insurmountable bitch in the blink of an eye, the once fair and wholesome roles of their relationship have forever changed. From now until death do they part, the wife can emotionally stab and lash out at her husband anytime she wants. Her abusive actions, wholly justified by his past discretions, end up being far more destructive to him over time than he could have ever imagined.

The thing is, though, that all this deceitful chaos happens behind closed doors. Always trying to maintain the public image of the blessed, healthy union that they once had, their hate for each other is treated like a dirty little secret around all their family and friends. Those that can see through this charade—through the false narrative of everlasting inner peace and happiness—know that the empty illusion won't last for long.

Sadly, nothing ever does.

One evening, while the same wife is out socially drinking with friends, she clumsily blurts out the awful truth of her marriage. Through mascara-laced tears, she drags out their dirty laundry—the lies, affairs, and verbal abuse—and lays it all out. Her friends, confused by this sudden admission, at first chalk up the emotional outburst to the rapid alcohol consumption that night. But when the wife continues to cry and sob about her personal woes, they know that her words were true. After getting her to calm down, her friends share with her the obvious bad news.

"Ugh, girl, you need to dump his ass!"

"Yeah! Once a cheat, always a cheat. Trust me."

"Don't feel bad for being cold to him. Hell, he's lucky you didn't snip off his nutsack for what he did behind your back! What an asshole!"

One by one, her friends rally to the sad woman's side and help put back the broken pieces of her shattered ego. The wife goes home after being built back up by her ill-informed friends and continues the lie. Nothing lost, nothing gained.

And so, the cycle continues.

The moral of this story is that it's far worse to pretend to be happy than to face your sadness head-on. You know that fairy tale where the prince rescues the damsel in distress, and then they ride off into the sunset to live happily ever after? Yeah, I hate to break it to you, but that's pretty much a big crock of shit. Unfortunately, most marriages are doomed from the beginning. There's no way around it; it is what is. All the signs of a disaster could be present from the get-go, but it wouldn't matter. Love is funny that way; it blurs common sense and lowers defenses unlike almost anything else.

Even now, I look around at all the honest, good people in the world that have to carry this burden and wonder why they all can't just find each other. Sadly, the answer to that seemingly simple question isn't an easy one to come by.

Sorry, not sorry.

Chapter 8
RUTHLESS DYSFUNCTION AT THE FAMILY FARM

We have already discussed the awful unpleasantries of having to put up with an unruly mother-in-law, but there are far more limbs on our respective crooked family trees. There's the dreaded sister-in-law, the cousins, the aunts, the uncles, and the rest of the goddamn family to consider. Admittedly, I don't have much experience in this field, but lucky for us, my friend Lesley—accomplished lawyer, mother of three, and recently divorced from her second husband, Tom—does.

Lesley met Tom while in high school, though they didn't actually start dating until way later in life. He was the star running back of the football team, and she a bookish, soft-spoken girl who was always in the background. Despite the fact that he wasn't the most attractive guy in school, Tom had the drive and determination to go places in life. Clumsy and dorkish around girls, he was nonetheless revered by most of his peers. Aside from being a pretty great football player, he was an A+ student and at the top of his graduating class. Lesley had no desires for the young heartthrob back then; her type was the dark-haired bad boy, not the all-American football star. Graduation came and went, and soon the two separated and went on their different paths in life.

Like most of the faces from her past, Tom was forgotten through the sands of time, buried under the new memories and events of Lesley's life.

A few years after the split from her first husband—I forget his name, but I remember that he was the bass player of a corny Van Halen cover band—Lesley was tired of sitting around watching Netflix and did something uncharacteristically brash. On a wild whim of fate and the pressing advice of a close girlfriend, she signed up for the popular dating app called Tinder. At first, Lesley was secretly mortified to be involved with such a filthy website that was so obviously designed for casual sex. But, in the end, the intense boredom outweighed the inner shame, and she decided to give the app an honest shot. While sifting through the endless profiles, she was surprised to have already matched with quite a few guys in her area. Some were great-looking, but lacked the attractive personality traits that she preferred. Then, after almost a month of no prosperous matches, it happened.

Like a blast from the past, Tom's picture appeared on her screen. Though greyer around the edges and definitely heavier than he used to be, he still resembled the awkward guy from high school. Despite the wide shoulders and the calm smile he sported in his profile photo, it was clear that the years had not exactly been kind to Tom. And, at the shock of seeing his long-forgotten face, her thumb accidentally slipped across the screen.

In a crucial error, Lesley had swiped right.

Oh shit! She freaked out in her head as the little checkmark notification blinked across the screen. *I didn't mean to do that! Nononono! Take it back! Take it back!*

But it was far too late for that. An automated message had been sent, and Tom would be notified that Lesley was interested in possibly hooking up with him. Although she was horrified by the mishap at first, she took a step back from the ledge and tried to think clearly.

Well, maybe this isn't a bad thing after all. I mean, maybe I should give him a chance regardless of the lack of physical chemistry between us. Who knows? He might turn out to be a pretty terrific guy.

Two short days later, she got a message back from Tom.

It should be said that Lesley described Tom as a painfully ordinary man: a bit on the tubby side and balding. The profile picture was clearly not an accurate reflection of who he was; filters had made him look better than he really did. But when they started corresponding, she was pleasantly surprised to discover that Tom was actually a great conversationalist. Charming and witty, they talked on the phone and texted for hours at a time. This eventually led to dinner plans. On the first date, Tom was very respectful, patiently listened to her stories, and even pulled out her chair. It was obvious that he wanted to make Lesley happy, and didn't once try to make an ill-timed sexual pass at her. And although Lesley knew she might never feel genuine physical attraction for Tom, she still thought he was a great guy and a wonderful person.

On her birthday the very next week, he took the plunge. Dropping to one knee in front of everyone at the party, he took a tiny black velvet box out of his pocket and held it up to a mystified Lesley.

"Lesley," Tom said as complete silence blanketed the crowded room around them. "Will you do me the honour of being my wife?"

They had known each other a little less than a month at this point, but the sincerity beaming from Tom's eyes was unavoidable. Not really wanting to say yes, but unable to resist the allure of the shiny Cartier diamond ring gleaming up at her from the open jewelry box in his hand, Lesley had no time to properly rationalize the immense request. The diamond ring, mixed with the hidden desire for lasting companionship, prompted her into mumbling a positive response.

Before she knew it, Lesley and Tom tied the knot.

Later that year, before the wedding date, they travelled across the country to meet Tom's parents. Tom was adamant that he wanted to tell his mother and father in person that they were engaged. The trip went okay until the couple arrived at the family farm out in the countryside. And—surprise, surprise—the parents weren't all that excited to meet Lesley. Of course, Tom was oblivious to the whole thing and was just happy to be back home with his family and wife-to-be. For him, it was the best of times.

For Lesley, it was pure, unadulterated hell.

And to make things that much more tense, Tom dropped a bombshell on her after the second day there.

"I booked you for a manicure/pedicure at a place downtown with my mom and sister," Tom said casually over breakfast. "Hope that's okay."

Mindful of the prying ears in the next room, she leaned over her cold cereal and quietly said, "I don't know, Tom. That's a lot of pressure. Might not be a good idea. Your family and I don't really know each other all that well. What will we even talk about?"

But within an hour, Tom personally dropped Lesley off at the spa in town. There, waiting curbside, was his mommy and sister with their plastic smiles and fake laughter. It was all for show, and the spectacle didn't last long after the three were alone. Once Tom drove off and left Lesley in their clutches, the sharpened knives came out. Like wicked stepsisters in a fairy tale, mother and daughter proceeded to verbally slander Lesley to random spa staff as if she wasn't even there.

"My poor son," Tom's grizzly mother said, her voice laced with forced sorrow. "He's gone and gotten himself mixed up with a real—how do I say this? A real loser. What was he thinking? My God, it's every mother's worst nightmare!"

This was followed by cackles of vindictive laughter to soften the words, but their true intent shone through.

Just as dumb but twice as loud, Tom's younger sister added, "OMG! I know! I mean, even someone like him can do better than... *ugh!* It's just...*ugh!*"

That day at the spa was long and painful. For almost two hours straight, they belittled and insulted her with no restraint. Although put off by their extreme rudeness, Lesley kept quiet about it out of respect for Tom. After all, they were his mother and sister, no matter how inexcusably vile. So, when Mommy Dearest and Ugly Sister-in-Law said they were far too busy for a following lunch date, Lesley was all too eager to agree. When it was time for Tom to come pick her up from the spa, Lesley feigned a weak smile and said her goodbyes. Dazed and confused by the awful encounter, she hurriedly climbed into the car with Tom and begged him to speed away.

On the long drive back to the country home, Lesley tried to explain to Tom what had transpired. But before she could even finish her harrowing tale, he was quick to interrupt.

"I'm sure they didn't mean it that way," Tom patiently said, his eyes never leaving the winding road ahead. "Sounds more like a simple misunderstanding to me. They could've been just trying to joke with you. Ya know, a little bit of sarcastic humour or something."

Suddenly enraged, Lesley glared viscously at Tom and snarled, "Look, I know what sarcasm is. Your mother and sister meant all the awful shit they were saying about me. I could tell." Seeing that he still wasn't taking her seriously, Lesley sternly added, "I'm serious, Tom. They really don't want us to get married. Doesn't that bother you at all?"

Right away, Tom got defensive. "They are just testing you, hun. Probably just want to make sure you'll stick around, is all. I know my mom doesn't want to see her baby boy get his heart broken again. And really, can you blame her?"

Lesley took an extra second to think about it and could honestly see Tom's point. Maybe his family was just being overly protective of him until the right amount of mutual trust had been gained—a maternal hazing of sorts. Coming to terms with that, Lesley kept her reservations to herself from then on.

And so, the wedding came and went. The newlyweds bought a house and moved in right away to start the rest of their happy life together. Or so they thought…

It wasn't long after the move that Lesley learned that Tom's entire family had no personal boundaries. They were persistently guilty of all the social taboos like drop-ins, walking into the house unannounced, and even taking food out of the fridge to take back to their own homes. Constant gossiping about Tom's ex-wife was an everyday occurrence as well, one that Lesley really hated. They seemed to have an opinion about everyone and everything, ill-informed though it might have been. They were also criminally cheap and proud of it. And when Lesley refused to be involved in their dirty gossip, they were quick to label her as an overbearing wife who controlled every element of Tom's existence. Soon, Lesley was begging Tom to help her deal with his toxic family members. But, just as before, he was reluctant to do anything of the sort.

"Please, Tom," Lesley pleaded, well at the end of her rope with all of the unmannerly chatter. "Please put our marriage first! How can you not see just how awful they all are?!"

We had all warned Lesley to try living with Tom as a test run before running off to get hitched, but she didn't listen. Drunk on newfound commitment, she instead followed her impulses. So, when Lesley inevitably told us that they were getting a divorce, my first impulse was to go in for a high five and order a celebratory bottle of Veuve Clicquot for the table.

"Don't get too happy," she warned me. "Tom is giving me a hard time about finalizing the separation agreement. I overheard him talking to his mother on the phone the other night and she's really spearheading this whole shakedown, I can tell you that." Taking a hearty sip from her cocktail, Lesley then looked me dead in the eye and added, "You know what I would do if I ever got my hands on a time machine?"

Taking only a moment to contemplate the age-old quandary, I evenly answered, "Go back and stop the wedding?"

"Nope," Lesley said, a sly smile creeping across her face. "I'd go back to that day at the spa and really let his mother and sister have it. That definitely would've made this whole mess all worthwhile."

For many of us with bills to pay, Monday morning comes far too quickly. After the weekend, our thoughts are consumed by the dread of rush hour commuting and the tragic reality of having to once again endure mindless idiots and bosses from hell! If this sounds at all familiar, then please read on.

The Corporate World

Chapter 9
THE CRAZY BITCH BOSS

Anyone who has managed to land that dream job after years of hard work knows just how rewarding that feeling of achievement can be. More than overwhelming pride, you feel a sense of release that comes with the conclusion to a chain of trying events that ultimately paid off nicely. Naturally, you'll celebrate the newfound success and give yourself a big ol' pat on the back.

Heed my words; the journey isn't over quite yet.

To put this in the simplest of terms, securing a great job is a lot like dating. You start off enjoying the thrill of the chase, running from interview to interview. But as soon as the wining and dining passes and you lock down the job, it happens.

Whether it's within the first month or the first year of employment, you will quickly become saddened by just how quickly things deteriorate. You will soon find that there has been a great misrepresentation of the proposed job title, a real bait and switch. And as if that isn't enough to deal with, your position is mired in phony office politics. If you try to stay objective and fight the hierarchy, it will kick you all the way back to the unemployment line. But if you play along and do what's expected, then you stand a chance of climbing the corporate ladder to the top.

Or so *they* want you to think...

As driven and enterprising as I am, I revel in the pressure of a high-stakes interview. Seriously, the tense one-on-one meetings give me an opportunity to not only flex my long list of skill sets and achievements, but also to feel out management and get a vague idea of how they might run things on the inside. I like to come across as confident, but not braggy or off-putting, and I treat the steady Q and

A like a friendly chess match. Move by move, I steer my pieces across the board in hopes of landing a new and exciting career at the other end. Most times, I do such a good job in these interviews that the companies in question call me back within a few days and practically offer me the sun, the moon, and the stars to drop everything and join their team.

Check. Mate.

I don't mean to come off as overly smug by this admission; in truth, I am just as gullible as the next poor guy. Like an ignorant sap, I once trudged along in the stagnant waters of unemployment, searching for that one perfect company who would finally treat me right and value my hard work. And, being the innocent soul that I am, I've stepped in more than my fair share of carefully laid traps.

As I got older and achieved more personal success, I quickly became stifled by the limitations of every huge conglomerate that hired me. But, over and over again, there was a consistent problem. And whenever I saw something not working the way it should—a plan, method, or strategical action—and tried to voice my concerns about it to the guys upstairs, I was immediately hushed.

"Don't rock the boat and you'll fit in just fine," they'd say from beneath their furrowed brows and concentrated stares. And although the message was subtly crafted, the words between the lines were clear; the patriarchal infrastructure is not about to change its ways for anybody. If it works for the bigwigs at the top, then it works all the way back down the line. Case closed.

Once I arrive at this professional wall, I know that it's time to move on. I've always been like that. I want to do things with my life that are dynamic and enterprising, not subservient and corrupt. If there's one thing that I can't stand, it's having my creativity stifled by other people's mediocrity.

And so, the search continued.

I reworked my resume at least fifteen times to get every word and description exactly right. I wanted the next interviewer to read my long list of accomplishments and be so impressed that they hired me on the spot. A fantastical goal, I know, but it's still entirely possible. With my nearly flawless resume, I then shopped around a little more and eventually got another promising lead. Dressed to impress, I arrived at this prospective interview like a total boss. The living image of polished perfection, I could tell the second I walked into the boardroom that I had their full attention.

As I sat across the table from the interviewer—a sad-looking man in a faded three-piece suit—I could already visualize my new high-rise office and six-figure salary. With the kind of lucrative funding that this new position would offer, I could afford to buy a new Benz or another Hermes Birkin bag to add to my vast and detailed haute couture purse collection. Hell, I did some quick mental math and thought that I might even have been able to swing both. Nevertheless, I kept the fantasy at bay and composed myself. Smiling pleasantly, I thought, *You got this, girl. Just stick to your regular script, and you'll do just fine.*

Just as I had hoped, I landed the job. And within a month, I quit and started the whole process all over again.

⊱⊰

I once had a senior management position that, on paper, seemed to be a great fit for me, not to mention a good career move. However, after the first six months dragged by, I realized just how sadly mistaken I was. I've heard employers and recruiters alike mention that most potential candidates usually stretch the truth on their resumes, which personally I don't agree with. I think that most career-seekers are just trying to accentuate all their positive attributes, but others are just straight-up lying. I, on the other hand, have never put any such bullshit on a resume. Why? Well…because I don't have to.

I'm the real deal, baby.

Interestingly, what most recruiters and employers fail to acknowledge is that they themselves are to blame for this rampant dishonesty. They strive for the image of perfect organization, leadership, and perpetual drive from all applicants. If you don't have what they want, then it's tough titties for you. Goodbye, better luck next time.

The snake eats its own tale once again.

☙❧

The idea of a "picture-perfect" boss was presented to me when I was hired for my most recent position.

The interview for the job was not at all what I had initially expected. The panelists conducting the interview appeared distracted, almost disinterested with the process—as most HR people are. But, regardless of this lackluster reception from the corporate peanut gallery, I put on a stunning show. Two days later, I got a call from one of the interviewers.

"I presume you're still interested in the position?" he asked, his voice still holding the same sleepy disdain from a few days prior. Of course, I said I was, and he told me the job was mine—on one condition. "The hiring director and company VP would like to meet with you in a...um...less formal setting. How does a lunch meeting for tomorrow afternoon sound?"

Again, I adamantly said yes and grabbed a pen and paper to scribble down the address and time for the meeting. Although the request struck me as kind of odd for a new hire, I was still excited at the prospect of making big connections.

At least, I was at the time...

When I arrived at the quaint yet elegant restaurant, I braced myself at the wide glass doors. Standing on the outside looking in, I took one last deep breath.

Remember, there's no need to sell yourself; the job is practically yours. Just go in there and do what you do. All right, time to make some magic happen.

Once introduced to my party, we quickly sat down at the small, candlelit table. As I looked over the drink menu, the man in the dark suit sitting to my left—the VP—turned to me and plainly said, "Essentially, this meeting is to confirm that you will fit in with the rest of the team back at the office. Comradery is very important to running a successful business."

Nodding, the man to my left—also wearing a crisp, dark suit, though he was much younger than the VP—added, "It's important for the department that every person on the floor is not only socially compatible, but also a necessary cog in the machine. Does that make sense to you?"

"Oh yes," I said, faking an intense interest even though I'd heard this same tired old speech at least a hundred different times before. "I completely understand and agree. Comradery is very important, sir."

The next two hours of the lunch went by rather smoothly. I laughed and gabbed with the suits, trading stock market war stories over expensive cocktails and appetizers. All in all, I felt good about the way the meeting went and left the restaurant knowing that I was a shoo-in for the position. My theory was confirmed the very next day. Not only did I get the call that I had the job, but I also got more benefits and a bigger salary than had been originally negotiated. Truly, I had come out on top. Right?

Wrong. So, so wrong.

Turned out, I had a little surprise waiting for me at the office in the form of the most rotten, cold-hearted bitch I have ever met: my new floor manager. Lower on the totem pole than the VP, but still retaining much more authority than I, Gretchen was and probably still is the vilest person I have ever met. I spent a couple of months enduring this soulless woman and her endless verbal lashings, not to mention her manic and emotionally unstable behaviour. There wasn't a single day that went by that I didn't see Gretchen completely lose her shit on some poor unsuspecting underling. Like a rabid junkyard pit bull, she'd latch onto some petty clerical issue and just start tearing away. Dark eyes void of any human light, Gretchen

THE BITCHOGRAPHIES

would practically foam at the mouth with rage at any minor inconvenience. Without a doubt, she was one hell of a nasty bitch.

For two long years, I bit my lip and tried to dodge Gretchen as often as I could. But the psychological warfare continued to escalate.

Soon, she started leaving cryptic messages on my voicemail after work hours and on the weekends. These—coupled with bizarre, rambling emails—started to border on something more like a suicide mission to gather intel on the Viet Cong. Needless to say, I put in my two weeks' notice and never looked back.

Thinking back now, there was one time that Gretchen left me a voicemail at like two in the morning on a Saturday that really made me laugh. I can't remember it verbatim, but it went a little something like:

"Hi, Vivienne, this is your boss…Gretchen. Listen, I was just in your office and noticed something of great concern. On your floor, about a foot away from your desk, I found a used disposable fork. Or, more specifically, spork. Now, there's no excuse for this. I just gave that team meeting on the importance of office cleanliness last Monday. Seriously, did it even occur to you that one of the high-ups might decide to come down to visit and see your filthy mess? Seriously, I'm disgusted right now. Well…all right then. See you on Monday. Remember what I said, or I will have to reprimand you the next time. Goodbye."

I can say now with absolute certainty that she was the pettiest woman alive.

Well…

Chapter 10
THE VAMPIRE AND THE SNAKE

I always get a good chuckle whenever I read articles or watch TV shows that perpetuate the myth that all office gossip occurs at the magical and mysterious water cooler. Trust me, the water coolers are always strategically located in the senior management area of any office building. You will never find them anywhere near the peons. During my most painful periods of employment, if I was ever desperate for a glass of water at work, I knew it would require a marathon walk.

Do I seriously want to risk jogging some VP's memory about a special project I need completed just for a cup of tepid water? They'll just try to flatter me and fill my head with half-hearted ego boosts in an attempt to get more work out of me. Why in the hell would I—or anybody—ever willingly sign up for any additional work? Pure madness!

As underpaid as I was at the time, what would have been the benefit of taking on the extra load at no added reward? That, my friends, is what I call a losing hand.

ॐ

When anyone describes the classic office gossip stereotype, it's always some nosey woman who is desperately trying to climb the corporate ladder. But, my friends, Romans and countrymen, this is a completely false and inaccurate presumption. Men, too, can be office gossips.

Granted, the gossip in question is often fairly benign. The type of rumours to watch out for are those of the dangerous and calculating variety, the ones designed to ruin another person's livelihood. But as much as management wants to pin the source of the rumours on the bored underlings, I've found that it is most often the figureheads of the company that do the most fatal shit-talking.

For them, talk was small—a game to be played with no direct side effects. Not to the ones spreading the gossip, anyway.

And then, there's the office Snake.

I call this sad excuse for a life-form "the Snake" because of how they tend to slither around and indistinguishably scope out their prey. Then, when the target's back is turned, they strike and subdue their prey, binding and constricting their image to death with half-baked rumours. As a natural predator, the Snake is extremely skilled in their proclivity for social camouflage. Potentially one of the most charming people you will ever meet, the Snake comes across as a kind and empathetic individual—someone you can trust. But underneath, there is a much different story to tell.

Initially they will do little, seemingly pointless favours to slowly lower your defenses—small things like bringing extra coffee or homemade cookies to your office. These friendly acts pave the way for more personal interactions. Like the slow leak of poison from a pointed fang, the Snake will attempt to erode your moral guard with confidential company information from their glory years at the office. Of course, the information that they share with you is readily accessible to anyone, but that doesn't matter. It's not the info, but the act itself that establishes trust.

Soon, you are conditioned to bend to their will.

Calculating and cunning, the Snake ensures appropriate alliances with all of the correct individuals in order to further elevate themselves on the corporate ladder. It is also of paramount importance that they are always publicly perceived as the "go-to person" around the office. With that title, they subtly establish a certain amount of control over their colleagues. Discreetly, the Snake gets others to do the dirty work, leaving their own hands clean and unblemished.

Lastly, the Snake creeps into your world and uncovers your

innermost weaknesses, cataloging them for later use. Once the eggs have been laid in the victim's psyche, it's only a matter of time until they hatch. And once the Snake has earned your trust, you make the fatal error of telling them all that you know.

But what you will soon find is that the very information that you have shared with the Snake is going to be used to destroy you and your achievements. This becomes alarmingly obvious as you watch the Snake take any and every opportunity to throw undeserving individuals under the bus. The Snake never truly reveals their authentic colours to anyone, but that doesn't matter. You are now fully acclimated to how office politics work, a secret master strategist among the other sheep. Using these craftily hidden skills you've acquired, you quickly learn how to utilize the Snake for your own purposes, flipping the game board on them. Eventually, once your needs are met, you expose the Snake for what they really are and eliminate them from the game.

Check. Mate.

I have gained something of a reputation for standing up for myself and staying true to what's intrinsically important. Undaunted by the consequences of my brash actions, I know that I still need to be able to look myself in the mirror each and every day and feel some measure of self-respect. I might not always like the options presented to me, but at least I have the freedom to make my own choices. I didn't back down from the Snake, and ultimately beat this particular one at their own game.

But even worse than a Snake is an office Vampire, aka a bloodsucker.

As I'm sure you know, vampires are leeches who drain other people's life force in order to nourish themselves. Well, I made a fatal error once in confiding in someone I thought was a mutual friend and colleague, but who turned out to be anything but. We would occasionally chat on the phone, openly discussing our personal lives and bitching about our incompetent bosses. But this supposed friend was working their own angle on not only me, but also on the senior VP of the company as well. A hostile takedown, if you will.

Before I fully realized this ugly fact, a very personal situation came up and I had no choice but to leave work and later go on medical leave. During my absence, I learned through the grapevine that the Vampire was getting awfully familiar and comfortable in my vacant office, pretending to have my role in the company. I also heard around this time that they were lining themselves up for a promotion—one that could create a very real problem for me. Obviously, this Vampire was gunning hard for my position while I wasn't there to defend myself. Then, a couple of weeks into my medical leave, I got an odd message on my voicemail.

"Hey, this is (Vampire). Hope you're doing well. Listen...I was wondering...would you mind giving me some advice? I got an interview coming up and could really use some mentoring. And I thought, who better than Viv to help me out? Anyway, hope to hear from you soon! Bye!"

Ignoring the message, I took some time to think about the dishonest proposal. I was emotionally hurt by the backstabbing at the time, jaded by past acts of similar treachery. This Vampire made me question everyone around me, forcing me to wonder if I could ever trust another colleague again. After a month of painful recuperation, both physical and emotional, I made a landmark decision. It was officially time for a change. As I prepared my resignation letter, I recognized that I wanted something more than what I already had. It was time to take a leap of faith, and to start betting on myself instead of the house.

Chapter 11

THE HOBBIT

When I was young(er) and full of promise, I hoped that one day I would hold a managerial position at a great company. As part of my career development, I longed for a chance to showcase my talents by optimizing my strengths, thereby inspiring a team of professionals to deliver above-average quotas.

I suppose, in retrospect, this desire to be a great leader was ingrained in me from an early age, and became much more prominent after I graduated from university. When I first entered the corporate world, becoming a manager seemed like part of my natural career progression. After all the exams that I wrote, all the extra time I spent committing myself to charitable causes, I expected to be rewarded with some form of an advancement opportunity or a pay raise. I worked ridiculous hours and spent an enormous amount of time endlessly stroking senior management egos—a much-needed survival tool when navigating the field of corporate business. I had no choice but to acquiesce to requests from the high-ups, even when I knew they were crap and made no apparent sense, and endured an army of terrible bosses. I finally reached the point in my career where I felt that I had "made it."

I'd like you now to consider the following situation.

It's the first day of your brand-new job. You feel apprehensive and overwhelmed, but obviously excited by the vast opportunities that lie ahead. You have been fundamentally empowered to make substantial changes to a poorly functioning department that has become systematically inept over time. In essence, your new boss has surrendered the keys to the kingdom, and your will is now considered his own. So, why would you be nervous?

You are a replacement, the direct result of your predecessor's termination for lack of competence. Coincidentally enough, their involuntary departure was somewhat clandestine in nature. You are not aware of all the specific details surrounding the situation, but you have gathered enough information from office gossip. Either way, the title and glory are now yours.

In order for your transition to go smoothly, your big boss has flown in from corporate to spend some quality time with you and to personally introduce you to your team.

"Tell the team a little bit about yourself," the big boss says while the other members of the office crowd around you. You are initially hesitant to say anything, thrown off by the negative vibes emanating within the fluorescent-stained room. "Don't be shy. Just tell us something about your education, personal experiences. Whatever you feel comfortable sharing with the team."

Now, you have never been one of those completely neurotic people, and are instead more on the understated, reserved and quiet side. You personally believe that there are way too many egomaniacs in the workplace already, and it's better not to add to the pool. It's rather unfortunate that when offer letters are prepared, there is not a section of the contract that informs people that all egos need to be checked at the door!

As you start to speak to the surrounding group, cracking some light jokes and sharing a few anecdotes, your eyes are immediately drawn to a curious individual standing toward the back. You watch with great disgust as they scribble down your every word on a yellow notepad they have clenched in one hand. Without letting your irritation show, you continue to look around at the team members and remind them that this is not a formal conversation and you will be meeting with each of them individually, one-on-one. This does nothing to dissuade the sacred scribe in the back. So, you quickly change your strategy and ask each of the team members to take turns describing a little bit about themselves, too. As one person at the end of the line kicks things off, you focus again on the scribe—who is still taking notes.

Suddenly, it's the scribe's turn to speak.

As you watch the man lower his notepad and speak in a small, mousy voice, a funny image suddenly pops into your head. This guy reminds you of a hobbit—a creature from Tolkien's fantasy world that roams the foothills of mountainsides and mystical forests. Once the connection is made in your head, you have no idea how you will ever take this man seriously again. And as he continues to drone on and on about himself, you observe the pained look on each of the team members' faces. But, even more disturbingly, you observe that the big boss is smiling and stroking his ego! Panic immediately sets in. Then, you must ask yourself if you're really up for this challenge. Can you manage a middle-aged, self-righteous, little man with hairy knuckles? Suddenly, you're not sure if you really want this job anymore, but there's no other choice. Boldly, you turn the other cheek and press onward—consequences be damned.

As the days turn to months, your tolerance level for the Hobbit's annoying antics has lowered to dangerous depths. You have established a reputation in the workplace as being blunt and straightforward. You make decisions expeditiously, which has quickly garnered support and respect from your co-workers and customers. However, there is one small issue, one wrinkle in your new position: the Hobbit. He continuously tries your patience. Disrespectful, rude and unkind, his exaggerated self-importance and ridiculous, irrelevant opinions interrupt productivity on a daily basis. You've asked him on multiple occasions to curb the negative commentary, but he doesn't really care what you have to say. He just smiles at you and says what he thinks you want to hear. After months of documenting his unexceptional behaviour and then turning it over to corporate, the floating heads at the top send down a verdict that boils down to a basic conclusion.

We understand your concerns. But honey, we just don't give a damn.

Basically, no matter how rude or inappropriate the Hobbit's behaviour gets, he's been deemed fundamentally important to day-to-day operations.

Later on, due to a personal event, you are off work for a period of time. Before you return, your boss contacts you and reminds you that, despite your concerns and reservations about the Hobbit, you are going to have to "make it work." No matter what happens, you are expected to swallow your pride and work with the resources that are available. Clearly, the higher-ups are not interested in the Hobbit's deficiencies and do not believe there is a need to remediate him. Whether you like it or not, the Hobbit is here to stay.

You decide before your official return to work that you will do as the boss asks, and you extend an olive branch by inviting the Hobbit out to a casual lunch. Although it goes against your better judgment, you know that it's the only way to make things work and hope to solidify some kind of mutual bond.

Immediately, he decides to tell you about how you're not respected by any of your co-workers and, in fact, are a bimbo! Before the little, ungrateful man can spew any more verbal sewage, you stop him dead in his tracks. With great restraint and poise, you gently remind him that you are his superior, and no matter what corporate says, his ass belongs to you.

After your lunch from hell, you know that this company will never be a good fit. From here, you start the journey all over again.

Rinse. Lather. Repeat.

Chapter 12
THE OPPORTUNIST

You have seen him in action: the silver-tongued pro that would make any political PR agent proud. He feigns interest in the plight of the proletariat, while he secretly pines for the opportunity to play with the bourgeois in upper management. Please make no mistake; the game of opportunism is not new to him. He's cunning, and he needs to have his name immortalized on the boardroom door and sit in the large corner office fit for a corporate tsar. You cringe at the very thought of him wallowing in the big leagues; he is arrogant, aggressive, and most likely a misogynistic pig.

You tolerate him in the boardroom, but pity his wife for what she must endure in the bedroom. You also pity any poor co-worker that has to report to him. Scientifically known as "passive-aggressive," he is a devious breed of spineless primate. As a survival tactic, he makes sure that his power plays are never called into question. He treats the staff around him like indentured servants whose honest opinions are not welcome, even when he asks for them. He thinks they are disposable, and has no qualms about using them up.

One fearless person in the organization sees through him. He sees her as his only true rival, a real threat who has influence and the power of popularity on her side. She is known as the keeper of secrets and the safe harbor, and will seek out justice for those who have been wronged. She's the white queen on the chessboard, and the Opportunist can't stand her one damn bit.

He knows that the corner office and the nameplate on the door are meant to be his, but she needs to be silenced before he can get them. One rumour at a time, he initially tries to destroy her on the battlefield, but fails miserably. Then he tries to discredit her through open warfare; to his dismay, this doesn't yield the results he needs. Frustrated and at a loss as to what he should do next, he almost gives up…until his wife suggests befriending her. She is far too dignified and polite to refuse him, after all.

He cracks his knuckles and tries to play her like a piano. He texts, he calls, he visits, and he shares his secrets in an attempt to show his human side. He thinks she is like putty in his hands to mold.

After his endless hours of laying the groundwork, the announcement is sent to the executive team. He has made it. He is getting the corner office and the nameplate. Unlike the white queen, his next course of action will be focused on settling scores; it's time to put everyone who wronged him in their places.

The white queen is his first target. The blame and shame tactic is implemented immediately. He nitpicks everything about her, trying to throw her off her game. He attacks her character and criticizes her work both publicly and privately. He makes desperate attempts at extinguishing her light and her fire, and is tireless in his quest to remove her from his kingdom. Time and time again, he crosses the line, and one day she decides she has had enough.

She sends him a note and calls his bluff. Always five steps ahead of him and his silly little games, she has had a checkmate move lined up for weeks. The office and the nameplate aren't important to her. All she ever wanted was to make a difference and be respected.

The Opportunist has violated the professional code countless times. He's miserable, fueled by vengeance and the need to always be right. He can stay put in his little office, surrounded by his ass-kissers and talentless yes-men, and imprisoned by the opinions and approval of the bourgeois. She will be the tsarina who is unafraid of falling on her sword, living in a perpetual state of freedom. The game will end because she does not want or need such silly, unimportant fools fucking with her head!

Chapter 13
SENIOR MANAGEMENT

Have you ever wondered how some seemingly ignorant individuals manage to occupy the lucrative roles of senior manager, CEO, COO, VP, or CFO? I must confess that after suffering through a thousand forced conversations with senior management idiots, it gets harder and harder for me to find any respect for them. More often than not, these essential "leaders" are not company assets, but liabilities. As I sit here now, I continue to try and fathom how such obviously incompetent dumbasses manage to slop their way to the top of a corporate ladder, but I just can't make any sense of it. For the sake of conversation, I have come up with a list of possibilities as to how this conundrum might have happened.

1. The moron in question may be directly related to someone already established in the company hierarchy (father is a CEO or VP and hands them the job on a silver platter).
2. They may be a phenomenal liar, schmoozing and ass-kissing anybody who will help them cut all the way to the front of the line. This tactic usually works well, though I can't say that I would ever stoop this low for a raise. Pretty pathetic, really.
3. They are a master manipulator, a human puppeteer of sorts who prays on the weak-minded and socially inept minions around the office. Like little ducks, they line up in a neat row on their command. Usually possessing great intellect but poor self-esteem, the minion is eager to do the project work for the puppeteer, who will inevitably take all the credit for the hard work and effort put in. The minion doesn't challenge the puppeteer due to their docile nature. And, honestly, who would

believe them if they tried to tattle? They lack all the suave social graces and political astuteness that the puppeteer readily possesses, making them appear to senior management like they're outwardly unapproachable and uncredited. Stuck in limbo, the minion is doomed to do the bidding of the puppeteer, or risk being psychologically tormented on a daily basis.

If you seriously consider these options, can you really blame them for taking the easy way out and just playing along?

Come to think of it, most of the high-level management that I have had the displeasure of working with have fit nicely into these three descriptions. They are almost never worthy of the respected position they hold, and their perceived professional magnitude and influence far outweighing their actual skill set. You would think that, at the very least, they would possess some kind of special qualities that would justify collecting such a large paycheque. You would think that they'd be goal-oriented, confident, forward-thinking, inspiring, charismatic, open-minded and motivated—just to name a few. However, as I compile a mental list of my past experiences with these supposed "giants of industry," I can't think of a single one that has ever struck me as anything other than dangerously incompetent and piggish. And while I find it almost impossible sometimes to keep my honest opinions to myself, I've learned to stay tight-lipped when forced to work around these clowns. In the end, they still hold a substantial amount of power over my position; their ability to fire me and toss my ass out onto the curb is very persuasive. So, to save my bank account, I shut my mouth and allow them to display their stupidity for all to see.

Hey, not my problem.

A while back, I once worked in upper management with a ruthless despot. To be completely frank, the man was utterly banal, prickly, rude, and unnecessarily demanding. Every single day, he would send curt emails to the rest of the team, demanding we drop everything and address some project he'd decided to hatch at the last possible second.

I get it; there is an essential rank and order to every organization that drives the business forward, a chain of command. So, when I'm asked by a superior to do something, no matter how ridiculous and trivial it may seem to me at the time, I get it done. That's what I'm getting paid to do, isn't it? However, I noticed there were some employees within the organization that required a warm, sentimental exchange before having orders aggressively barked at them. In their minds, once a task had been requested or completed, there should have been some kind of acknowledgement to follow. Something like, "Hey, great job!" or "Keep 'em comin'!" But, sadly, many times there was no gratitude to be had—only begrudging silence and expected outcomes.

A good leader—someone who is capable of optimizing and mobilizing their resources and team to obtain an optimal output—traditionally takes constructive criticism and learns from it. From this selflessness, they will gain the trust of their team. Next will come respect and then the rewards for their hard work. But apparently, some managers think it's a better idea to go the other way. Yeah, fear works to get what you want at first, but that always changes.

For example, my direct superior came up to my office bitching and complaining about the poor morale around the office. Deathly quiet, the cubicles looked more like flimsy mausoleums with listless zombies tucked away inside. He was completely ignorant to the cause of this mass distress, though I could think of a few reasons. At the time of his unannounced intrusion, I was drinking my usual morning coffee—a sanctimonious ritual that I normally did in the quiet solitude of my office. Unfortunately for me, the kind of awareness it would take to recognize this was clearly not this man's forte.

If he had bothered to pay attention during all the company training courses, he would've realized that you can't kick people around and then expect them to be happy about it. It never looks good when a corporation has senior management that just wanders the hallways and acts like they are better than everyone. Belittling and chastising someone based on their job titles is an awfully shitty thing to do. Everyone knows that the people on the bottom are the ones that really keep the company running, not those lazy senior managers in their luxury suites. Without the peons—the minions and proles—there would be no title and fancy corner office to help inflate their massive egos.

They would be just like everyone else: regular people.

In my personal opinion, it is of critical importance to validate, acknowledge and respect the people around you—no matter how many digits are on their respective paycheques. This couldn't be more important for those with whom you have a direct reporting relationship at work. Now, I don't expect that my boss will remember all the finite details that make up my unique personality. And you know what? That's okay. All that I ask is that he show me a shred of respect by remembering my name and keeping his wandering eyes off my cleavage. Is that so much to ask? I think not.

&

I personally knew a VP who was a very attractive, debonair man. He was well aware of this and not ashamed to speak of it. During my time under him (no, not *that* way), I had heard dozens of rumours about his more...um...*wild* ways. Let's just say there was talk of several steamy office romances, all of which tied back to this one married man with a cushy position as company VP. I had a lot of daily, personal interaction with this VP and noticed that he made a lot of sexual inferences during casual conversations with me. At the time, I thought it was just his way of being chummy and treating me like just one of the "bros." But over time, I realized that it was anything but chummy. Slowly, the talk got more aggressive—more graphic and suggestive. Clearly, this VP had his eye set on me to be next in his long line of office flings.

As soon as I put the pieces together, I wanted to tell him outright that I was not interested in him in any way, shape or form. Well, really I wanted to punch that sentiment right into his finely chiseled nose, but thought that might be a little too uncivil. I *am* a sophisticated and expensive lady, after all.

For Christ's sake, you're a married man! I could almost see myself saying right to his smug face, my imagination projecting what my lack of courage would not allow. *It's absolutely disgusting to see how you let your wife fawn all over you at Christmas parties while the rest of us know what kind of depraved perv you really are when she isn't around. Don't you have any shame, any guilt for what you do behind her back? No, I didn't think you did, you sick, sick man. You know, I've been tempted on several occasions to walk right up to her and ask if she knows that her husband is a raging man-whore. I doubt she does, but she should. Know this, you overinflated windbag; I have no desire to sleep my way to the top of this company. So, go ahead and put your dick back in your pants and don't ever talk to me like this ever again!*

But, as usual, I kept a civil tongue and opted to say nothing at all. In the end, it was easier just to let it go. Anyway, time and a couple of sexual harassment lawsuits could do the rest for me.

❦

All she ever wanted was to make a difference and be respected. I always laugh inside when one of these "big dogs" wants to open up the sales floor and have an open discussion with the other employees. They always ask the same questions, expecting the same answers in return. Back and forth, the same predictable lines get spitballed across the room. Like being stuck in an unstoppable time loop in which you are forced to relive the same pointless team meeting until the sun burns out, the benign predictability of these things can be torturous.

In the fall of 2018, I was sitting in one of these useless town hall meetings, practically drooling from boredom, when an employee raised his hand. He wasn't one of the usual characters to pop up during the meetings. He was a shy lad who wore glasses with thick frames and had pockmarked skin. When the manager finally noticed him and stopped talking, the man meekly stood up from his folding chair and said, "I have a suggestion...well, more of a comment, concerning the hazardous waste problem being reported at our coastal production plants."

Immediately, the entire room went completely silent. This wasn't part of the typical script, causing a ripple of tension to pierce through the crowd.

Clearing his throat and obviously gathering his thoughts, the manager in charge of the meeting quickly offered a corny smile to the earnest man and pleasantly responded, "That's great! But why don't you take a mental note on it and save that one for the end of the meeting? Thanks! Okay, what were we talking about?"

He then went on to spew a nonstop flow of verbal diarrhea for the next forty-five minutes about proper breakroom etiquette. After explaining for the third time the importance of cleaning the microwave after every use, the meeting was adjourned. When we were all corralled back to our cubicles, I looked over my shoulder and saw the look of crushing disappointment pulling on the one employee's face who thought his opinions would finally be heard. Hopes ruined, he slunk back to his lonely cubicle and never spoke up in one of those meetings ever again.

Not today, little buddy. Not ever.

Due to such pompous displays from people like the cocky VP I just described, employees quickly learn that they are better off just keeping their honest opinions to themselves. Even if their ideas are really innovative and may even benefit the company, it still isn't worth the trouble. So, with no incentive to workshop new and interesting ideas, a creative and morale stagnation occurs—one that will eventually lead to an internal collapse of the team spirit. This VP had clearly demonstrated that employee opinions are only valuable if they already aligned with his way of thinking. Oh, and also if they didn't cost the company any money to implement. To them, the best ideas are free, or are, at the very least, tax-deductible. Anything else is just wasteful.

On the flip side of that same dilemma, being heard by your boss can have some seriously negative consequences attached. Let's say you have a great idea that could make the company millions, so you bring it to your direct manager. Good, right? Wrong. Management will not only hear out your great ideas, they will also steal them. Like bandits in the night, they erase your name and scribble in their own in all the right places before running the idea straight to the top, all the while boasting their own creative genius for coming up with it. These phony shot callers don't seem to care that some poor sap spent hours—possibly days—designing and planning a profitable tool just to have it stolen from right under their noses by someone they are supposed to be able to trust.

I recall that same company telling employees one year that their Christmas pay raises would be capped due to low profit margins. What this really meant was:

"Sorry, guys. All us fat cats here at the top have to pull in at least eight figures apiece. So, the rest of you down there will just have to take the scraps we give you and be happy about it. M'kay? Thanks for the hard work—now scram!"

What greedy, lowlife bastards like this need to understand is that what keeps their company propped up and running isn't them, but all the little people at the bottom. Throughout the entire history of economic infrastructure, the airheads at the top are only good for signing papers and shaking hands. The real work—the blood, sweat and tears that grease the wheels of an economy—all comes from those downstairs, for they are the real spine of the operation. There's a slogan that comes to my mind when I think about this ironic class structure, one crafted for a steel manufacturer in the early nineteenth century.

"Our product is steel, but our strength is people."

My final advice to senior management is to be unafraid to acknowledge your co-workers in the office hallways and breakrooms. Don't be afraid to recognize their efforts and strengths, their struggles and tribulations. Not only will you gain their respect by doing this, but you will boost good vibes for the entire team. Oh, and maybe try to remember their names from time to time.

    Just a thought.

Chapter 14
SERIOUSLY? ARE YOU KIDDING ME RIGHT NOW?!

Unfortunately, there are times in the workplace when we are forced to associate and endure certain individuals that we would not normally interact with in any other capacity. To put it in terms that I find to be more nice than accurate, these employees have been vaguely described as "oddly mannered, but well-meaning."

Yeah, okay...

At one of the many jobs I've had the pleasure of holding, I received an urgent email from one of my colleagues. In the message—which was pinned all over with red flags—he practically begged me for my assistance on a special project he had been assigned to head. Apparently, I needed to call him at his office ASAP to discuss the details. He was one of those seasoned middle manager types whose mindset was stuck in the misogynistic 1960s era of business. In his eyes, women were not equal to men, and never would be. Not only morally superior, he also thought himself to be quite the big shot. A real baller, if you know what I mean. This guy honestly tried to say he was close friends with the company's CEO. I don't care who you are; accidentally meeting up on a golf course one time doesn't automatically make two people friends. It just doesn't work like that. And even though he was only a middle manager, this guy saw himself as a tsar among other royalty. But if you ask me, he was more like King Shit of Turd Island. To add to this string of delusionary thinking, this guy was under the impression that I actually cared about his ideas and commentaries—as if!

But then again, he probably thought that about anybody unfortunate enough to get locked into a conversation with him.

Honestly, I procrastinated making the dreaded phone call to his office, but I knew the one-sided conversation was unavoidable. One way or another, he would find me, so it was best to just call and get the whole thing over with. Pausing to let out a troubled sigh, I picked up the phone at the edge of my desk and dialed his extension. Against every chanting wish in my head, the other end began to ring softly.

"Thank God, it's you!" he cheered, having picked up the phone after only the second ring. Voice brimming with tightly wound panic, he didn't wait for my response before blabbering, "Listen, you gotta come give me a hand with this layout, or Jeffries is gonna have my ass! I told him I would have it done by the end of the day, but I've hit a wall! Oh man, if Sullivan finds out the report isn't finished, we'll both be in hot water, friend. Remember, you said last week that if I needed any help on this that I just had to ask. So, technically, we're both involved—"

Sitting at my desk, eyes rolling so hard I thought they might fall right out of my skull and spin out the front door, I calmly interjected, "We? No, there's no *we* in this. Just you. It's your project, not mine. You waited until the absolute last minute to ask me for help. That's on you, *friend*. If you drop the ball, my hands are clean."

"Sweetie," he purred, laying on that phony executive charm extra thick. "Let's be rational here. You know how these things go; you scratch my back, and I scratch yours. Now, do you wanna help me out, or do you wanna—"

Without even the slightest hesitation, I let out a disappointed sigh and evenly responded, "No, not this time. Sorry, but I'm way too busy right now. You will have to figure this one out on your own." Remembering something of urgency on my end, I dug out a bundle of papers from the financing folder on my desk and added, "But while I've got you on the phone, I need to talk to you about these expense reports from last month." The line went deathly silent then, so that only a faint buzz of the wires could be heard. Sensing that I had him against the ropes, I decided to double down and really press him for some answers. "Are you aware that you took almost three thousand dollars of the company's spending budget?" When I was met with more tense silence, I chuckled a little and added, "I don't have the time, the energy, or the patience to play a game of twenty questions with you right now. Whether you decide to answer me or not, I will do a follow-up report regarding these suspicious MasterCard charges to a place called...The Jiggly Kittens. I looked up the address, and it appears to be a strip club down by the airport. Sound familiar to you?"

"W-wait just a damn minute," he finally croaked, voice stretched like the tight skin of a drum. "I-I can explain that. The cards...um... they must've...ah...oh! They must've got mixed up in my wallet when I was out on the town. Yeah, I meant to use my own card, that's it. Simple mistake." Forcing a nervous laugh, he clumsily added, "Guess I was having a little too much fun and wasn't paying attention. Sorry 'bout that."

An obvious lie, but I still patiently held my tongue and waited until he was done stammering to speak.

"While I have no doubt that you had a good time at The Jiggly Kittens, I don't think that Sullivan will consider lap dances to be a justifiable business expense. No, I don't think he would like this at all."

His tone shifted to one of bitter disdain as he suddenly lashed out like a hurt badger with its back pressed to a tree and growled, "Go right ahead and tell Sullivan. We'll laugh about it later while we're out fishing on his forty-foot yacht! I told you it was a mistake, bitch, so let's just leave it at that!"

I'm sure he expected to trick me into losing my temper or ending the call in shock. Instead, I paused for a collective moment and then casually said, "Regardless of who you may or may not be friends with, you still need to have a personal cheque on my desk by the end of the day that covers all these expenses. Or else..."

There was a sharp grunt from the other end, as if he were choking on his own breath. Attempting to call my bluff, he emitted another snotty laugh before slyly asking, "Oh yeah? Or else what? What the hell are *you* going to do to *me*? Huh? Let's hear it, tough guy."

Unperturbed by his continued razzing, I smiled and said, "Or else I'm taking this receipt right up to Sullivan's office myself. Together, we will run through every single detail of every...single...charge. Sounds fair, yes?"

In a half-hearted last attempt to leverage any pity I might have had for him, he issued a painful sigh and weakly mumbled, "All right...I didn't want to tell you this...but I've been super sick over the past holiday. Pardon my French, but I spent most of the weekend brewin' up some hot iced tea in the toilet—if you catch my drift—"

"Oh God, stop! I don't need to hear that!" I gasped, thoroughly disgusted by the mental image he'd forced into my head. Desperately needing to change the subject, I reiterated, "Just get the cheque to my desk before five, okay? No excuses. And make sure the cash by date is for today—" All of a sudden, an odd noise stopped me in my tracks. Like the steady drip of water falling from a great height, a *click...click...click* could be heard over the receiver. Concerned that it might be another problem with the newly installed phone operating system, I asked, "Did you hear that? Something must be wrong with my phone or something. It got glitchy there for a second."

"Noise? Nah, that's me," he said ever-so-carelessly. Again, I could hear the *click...click*. This time, I realized that it was actually coming from his end of the call. "I am just clipping my toenails at my desk right now."

As any sane, reasonable person would be in response to such a nauseating admittance, I was left totally speechless. How could I possibly comment or respond to that with anything other than putrid gagging? Ugh! *In your office?! Oh my God, what a pig!*

At that moment, I made a mental note to never step anywhere near his office ever again. God only knew what other deplorable acts went down in there.

Honestly, I would rather not know.

There are always certain employees that think that they are more entitled than everyone around them. These individuals either don't know or don't care that they are just as disposable as the next guy. To them, they are without question the best in show—even if their only real duty is to run the office copier. In short, these people have big egos, but small paychecks.

An unbalanced ego.

Such was the case with these two idiot sticks that I had to discipline one time when I was employed as an HR representative. I know, I know. Please don't judge me too harshly.

Anyway, these two morons were always barging into my office and complaining about this and that and everything else. If one of them happened to fart too loudly, the other took it as nothing less than assault. Back and forth, they flooded my inbox with pseudo complaints about company harassment and bullying. After two months of having to hear this incessant bellyaching, I finally decided enough was enough and pulled them both into my office. Predictably, the two middle-aged men came in acting overly defensive right off the bat, and were completely hostile toward one another no matter what was said. For a solid ten minutes, they bickered like old ninnies about all the petty little things they hated about each other.

"You're too loud when you eat your lunch at your desk!" one screeched, his puffy face redder than a crab apple. "You know I'm right next to you, trying to work, but *nooo*, you don't care! In fact, I think you do it on purpose just to mess with me!"

The other man, just as spiteful and undignified as the first, angrily rebutted, "Whatever, you don't know what the hell you're talking about. You're the one who's always stinking up the microwave in the breakroom with that burnt popcorn! Learn to use the popcorn button, moron. It's not that hard!"

This lunacy would've gone on and on until they were at clawing at each other's throats if I hadn't stepped in and curtly said, "I don't know what you two think my job entails, but I can tell you that it is not to babysit a couple of weak-minded man-babies who can't settle their own personal affairs." With my heated glare barreling down on both of them from across my desk, I slowly leaned forward in my chair and added, "Is that what you two are? A couple of stupid man-babies? Hmm?"

Obviously trying to protect their pride, they both reflexively straightened up in their chairs and adamantly shook their heads in denial of the shameful title, the bitter feud forgotten.

"That's good," I commented with a hard smile, pleased by their subservient demeanor. "Because if either of you wastes a second more of my precious time with this petty bullshit, I'll see to it that you both never step foot in this building again unless it's to clean out your desks. Are we clear?"

Like timid bobblehead figurines, they frantically nodded in agreement before quickly scuttling off to hide in their cubicles. After they were gone from my sight, I closed my office door and laughed to myself a little bit about the whole situation. There was no way they could ever know this, but I wouldn't have actually gone through with getting them fired.

Come on. I'm not *that* cruel.

Oh, here's another personal favourite of mine.

On Christmas Eve, I was instructed by my boss to email her all the quarterly spreadsheets. I sneered, knowing full well that nobody would ever look at these before New Year's Day unless it was for kindling! Normally I wouldn't care, but on this very occasion, I did! It was Christmas Eve, and the last day of shopping for the delinquents who'd failed to buy their last few things. This boss of mine knew that I didn't have a proper internet connection and that this would take hours on end!

The drive to the office alone took nearly two hours due to a freak snowstorm that started just after I left my house. Snowdrifts blanketed the roads and blurred the lines all around my car. Unable to see more than two feet in front of my bumper, I was forced to drive at a snail's pace pretty much the whole way there. Eventually making it through the wintery tundra, I finally reached the office and sheltered myself inside. Within ten minutes, I had sent her the damn spreadsheets.

There, I tiredly thought, ready to get back to my family and continue with the festivities. *Now if she calls me again with any more favours, I don't have to feel bad about declining. I did my one good deed for the holiday season. That's enough for me.*

But as I was about to head out from the front lobby of the building to my car, my BlackBerry began to pulse and vibrate in my pocket. Expecting it to be one of the kids asking when I was going to be home, I quickly pulled it from my coat pocket and answered. But to my great dismay, it was my bitchy boss.

"Hey, got the papers," she said, not a hint of gratitude to be found in her authoritatively stony voice. "Do me a favor and don't file a mileage report for this. I don't want the extra paperwork on the holidays."

This then triggered a long, drawn-out story about her in-laws flying in from Chicago for the holidays.

Stifling my rage, I quickly put the call on mute, took the deepest breath I could, then held the phone out and screamed, "I got a better idea…why don't you go visit www.gofuckyourself.com! You stupid, selfish, whiny little bitch!"

My rage now properly depressurized, I gathered myself together and then took the call back off mute. Calmly, I listened to the rest of her nagging story with little fanfare.

When the boss finally ran out of hot air, she resignedly clucked her tongue and added, "Well, I should really be going now. Got a lot to do around the house. You know how it is, the stress of the holidays and whatnot. Perhaps you and your family could come visit our vacation home in Martha's Vineyard this spring. You would love it; it's so beautiful out there. Classy, too."

Fighting back a rising wave of angry nausea, I faked a pleasant tone and responded, "That sounds swell. I'll get back to you on that once I take a good look at my holiday schedule."

With that little white lie out of the way, the call was mercifully ended. Finally, I was free to go home and live my life.

Truth be told, there isn't enough money on the planet to compensate someone for having to deal with people who think and act like this woman did.

And yet, my story goes on.

Chapter 15
THE MILKSHAKE GIRL

There is another breed of animal in the office jungle, commonly known as the "Milkshake Girl." And much like the popular song, she genuinely thinks that her milkshake brings all the boys to the yard. And, of course, that it's much better than yours.

Despite this perceived advantage, she is grossly unqualified for the position that she holds within the company. But that grey area hardly ever seems to matter. Why? Well, first off, she always carries herself with an air of superiority—bossy and rude to her peers. This projects a false image of strength and control, convincing others that she is somebody to be reckoned with.

Secondly...well, let's be honest. She's probably banging a few of the managers on the side. I know it's a crude assumption, but I have seen it happen time and time again. Ya know, she only does it for the job security. And trust me, that is some of the best insurance you could possibly get when you're starting out in a big company. Now, you might be asking yourself how someone could coast so effortlessly through life as a human meat puppet while others toil away in obscurity. Honestly, no one really knows for sure, but I have an anecdote that might help explain this just a little bit.

Milkshake Girl started out at a huge Fortune 500 company in a rather modest position—daytime receptionist. But soon, some of the boys in ties around the office started to notice her. And why wouldn't they? She was young—in her early twenties—with plump, luscious lips and a sensual hourglass figure that could make even the hardest man smile with intrigue. Testing the waters, the boys took turns pushing the limits of decent conversation, their sexual innuendo and seemingly friendly touches becoming more rampant with each passing day. Desperately wanting to keep her new job, Milkshake Girl at first played along with the ambiguous flirting and teasing. Convinced that this was what she had to do to get ahead, she flirted right back and attempted to play the game herself. She wasn't going to be a victim, oh no. Milkshake Girl was going to use that same inappropriate attraction against them. Lining up their heads like steppingstones, she would cross the pond of fiscal success and come out dry on the other side.

Right away, her plan of deception worked perfectly.

Eventually, she became the object of affection for the company's CFO—a thrice-divorced, unattractive old man of Napoleonic height and a jiggly potbelly. Like Milkshake Girl, he, too, was dangerously incompetent. But unlike her, he had an almost endless amount of money to spend.

This, she liked.

Over time, Milkshake Girl became a despised figure to some within the company. They saw her for what she was: a gold digger. So, it was to everyone's great dismay that she received promotion after promotion for doing practically nothing. Well, if you didn't count keeping the CFO happy between the sheets. All ill manners aside, Milkshake Girl wasn't blessed with a high IQ or anything like that, just good genetics everywhere else. Regardless, the CFO was completely smitten with the young woman. Naturally, she wanted the world to see her achievements as well deserved, but some of her colleagues knew better than that.

The CFO's boss was a nice enough guy, but incredibly naive about these kinds of spicy matters. His preferred approach was to turn his back and pretend he didn't see a thing. Out of sight, out of mind. The best he could do was hope that the inappropriate fling between co-workers would wear itself through—ideally without any company interference that could lead to a messy HR issue. Or worse, a public lawsuit.

But it never did just go away like they wanted it to. It got much, much worse.

After being openly challenged by other employees about this inappropriate relationship with the much younger employee, the CFO became rather indignant. Without a hint of shame, he then spilled the beans on the whole affair—telling everyone all the juicy details that he'd promised Milkshake Girl he would never share. Within a week of the public confession, everyone and their mother knew the dirty little secret. Some serious damage control needed to take place, and fast. An ethics inquiry was shortly issued on the matter in an attempt to quell the growing chaos within the company's ranks.

From there, everything began to fall apart. But not for Milkshake Girl.

She knew full well that she was protected from any severe punishment. Because of her age and gender, she was able to convince everyone that the CFO unfairly pressured her into an intimate relationship. This ultimately shifted all blame onto the CFO, clearing her of any wrongdoing. After all, she was just a young woman, and he was a pervy old man who was supposed to know better. With his established position of power, he had lured her to the dark side and took advantage of her frail sensibilities—or so she wanted everyone to think. Clearly, Milkshake Girl was not at fault here. Case closed.

Draping the victim's cloak over herself, she could pretty much pick and choose her fate with impunity. Milkshake Girl could bully anyone in the company that threatened her lack of knowledge, lest they face her unquestionable wrath. Truly, a monster was born.

How could anyone knowingly allow this type of behaviour and unprofessionalism to exist in the workplace? It's just so shameful and wrong, not to mention unfair to the hardworking employees. The Milkshake Girl, though cruel at times, is a survivor, a self-made woman of sorts. Think about it; that nasty old man tried to take advantage of her and failed. Instead of getting the one-up on her, the tables were turned on him for a change.

A little bit of due justice, if you ask me.

Whether you think what she did to that CFO was wrong or right, one thing is certain, and that is that in a cutthroat business world,

THE BITCHOGRAPHIES

Milkshake Girl is smart to only look out for the one person that matters most.
    Herself.

Chapter 16
BULLIES IN THE BOARDROOM

As a woman sitting alongside the boys in the boardroom, I thought at one point that I had reached the top of the ladder. Not the very tippy-top, but pretty damn close. And if there was one girl that could shatter the age-old glass ceiling and claim a rightful chair at the top, it was sure as hell me. Even back then, I was an unstoppable force of nature when it came to my work, full of fiery passion and inertial energy. Of course, I could be a total bitch when it was required—a good asset to have in the tough corporate climate—but, really, I had no clue what I was getting myself into.

My first week in the bullpen, the boys were all fairly well behaved. But, like a subtle stench that has yet to fester, I could sense an underlying thread of resentment lingering in response to my presence. None of them had ever respected any of my opinions or ideas before I joined the team, and I didn't think that feeling had changed at all. Obviously, I had to do something to earn their respect, or I would always be the odd man out in every single meeting.

But in order to properly acclimate to the group, I would need to concentrate on winning over at least one of them first. With someone on my side, the rest might come around and realize that I wasn't all that bad. And maybe, over time, we might even grow to be a really great team. I knew some of them were jealous of me for getting into their exclusive little boys' club, but I didn't care about that. What I did care about was the fact that they would do whatever it took to annihilate my credibility if I didn't get them to accept me. I know that's a tad on the dramatic side, but I had been burned before and knew to be ready for the worst.

Over time, I felt them start to warm up to me a little. Conversations around the conference table became looser and less condescending. Little by little, I felt like I was carving out my own piece of the company pie. But this was so far from the truth.

It wasn't long before I became the subject of a series of malicious rumours around the office. Whispers of breakroom sex after hours started circulating. Without much thought, I linked the awful rumours back to my colleagues—the good ol' boys in the boardroom. Crushed, I had never felt so hurt and embarrassed before in my life. Being mislabelled as a home-wrecker and the company whore by my fake friends felt like a knife right to the gut. Every time I heard a whisper or saw a judgmental glare, that knife twisted further in. At first, I tried to laugh off the offensive nonsense, roll with the punches, and act as if none of it bothered me in the least. Well, that didn't last long.

Who would believe such tripe, anyway? They are so obviously rumours, just locker-room talk, I thought, still trying to be the bigger man about the whole thing.

But to my great dismay, many people around the office actually believed the raunchy sensationalism. Hook, line and sinker. Publicly shamed, I was then forced to navigate the office as if I had the scarlet letter tattooed across my forehead. The whispering and sniping—so loud sometimes that I couldn't help but hear—made me want to rage by the end of each workday.

Why me, though? What did I ever do to deserve this type of treatment?

And just as I was about to give in to my impulses and throw in the towel, it happened.

As a sign of good faith in light of everything that was happening, some of the boys from the boardroom invited me out for drinks one night after work. Stunned and very skeptical, I agreed to go. While at the bar, they graciously filled me in on the purpose of the intense teasing going on at the office.

"The rumours are nothing more than a form of initiation," one of them said over his beer. "It's a rite of passage, I guess. We all had to go through it when we started out upstairs. Just business as usual."

He and another co-worker exchanged a mischievous glance, clueing me in on their clumsy ruse rather quickly.

In total disbelief at the phony admittance of the abuse being just some mean initiation, I slammed down my drink and yelled, "Are you for real?! How is slut-shaming me behind my back an initiation? That's bullshit and you know it."

If I didn't need that job so badly at the time, I would've knocked his silly ass out and quit right then and there. Instead, I calmed myself down, kept my cool, and outwardly brushed it off as no big thing. But really, I was just biding my time…

A few weeks after that uncomfortable incident, the VP of sales dropped by my office to give me a powerful soliloquy about how he had had nothing to do with the rumours. Honestly, I wanted to puke in my mouth as soon as he started fumbling his way through a phony cover story.

"I-I don't know who it is," he guiltily insisted, "but it's not me. I swear. Why would I do that? Exactly, I wouldn't. It's just sick how disrespectful some people can be. Terrible."

Once he was sure I wasn't going to leap across my desk and bite his head off, he quickly left my office and went back to laugh it up with his buddies upstairs.

The bullying continued both in and out of the boardroom, with new players being constantly introduced to my long list of made-up "glory bangs." For months, I was propositioned on an almost daily basis, asked out for drinks I didn't want. There was also the blatant ogling, where men practically burned holes in my clothes with their unblinking stares. I complained about all of this to my HR rep, but my cries once again fell on deaf ears. Reaching the end of my rope, I started seeing a therapist outside of work to deal with the stress. When that didn't work, I began self-medicating with hard liquor. I did anything and everything I could in order to tolerate the constant degradation, devaluation and shame I felt every single day. Yes, the rumours hurt, but it was the fact that nobody cared how they made me feel that really got to me. And although this didn't qualify as physical abuse, it was still incredibly inhumane.

So, one cold September day, I told myself it was time for me to stop being scared and end the torture once and for all. Enough was enough; no person would ever take away my tiara again.

And so, I have worn it proudly—without fear or shame—ever since.

Every single day, I suspect that we all come into contact with a variety of individuals. Some of these interactions occur by choice and are pleasant and enjoyable in nature. However, there is another kind of contact that is unfortunate, dramatic, irritating, and, more often than not, painful.

People

Chapter 17
THE MELTED BARBIE

Up until recently, I never imagined that there could exist a human being that would deliberately turn themselves into the living carbon copy of a Barbie doll. When I was a little girl, I had no desire to play with plastic dolls that had bleached hair, unemotional faces, and an unattainably perfect body. As young as I was at the time, when my mother tried to buy me these dolls, it was my unshakable opinion that Barbie perpetuated a dangerous stereotype created and marketed to impressionable girls by sexist old men. It was unimportant for Barbie to be an intelligent, strong woman. Instead, they made her the quintessential bimbo. And really, that was the plan all along.

Even nowadays, I often get a chuckle out of Mattel's most recent media campaigns for the newer generation of dolls. Revamped for the socially conscious era, Barbie now represents the image of female success and prosperity. She's a positive role model. You know, what it should've been from day freakin' one. Anyhow, being the critically thinking individual that I am, I'd like to ask the manufacturer why Barbie is still physically flawless. Why isn't she representing more factions of real-life beauty?

Not all girls are blessed by the genetic lottery like Heidi Klum or some other equally beautiful model, so why push the idea that they are all capable of attaining it? To many, Barbie's image conjures up feelings of plastic fakeness—soulless and unfeeling. Like a Ziploc bag with straw hair, Barbie was once so morally and contextually thin that you could practically see right through her. The Barbie definition of beauty and the attainment of physical perfection doesn't work for everyone. Women and men alike determine what label they live by, whether it's the attainment of the self-imposed physical perfection or the acceptance of loving the skin you are in.

Sorry, not sorry.

With that said, I find it quite ironic that I would later meet one of these pseudo Barbie prototypes, except this wannabe Barbie was anything but perfect. A real rotten mamma, she was melted on both the inside and the outside; her character was just as fatally flawed as everyone else's. Refusing to take any kind of constructive criticism, this Barbie could never be held accountable for anything that she or her entourage did, no matter how heinous or cruel. As far as she was concerned, her way of doing things was the only way, despite the obvious fact that she was dumber than a sack of doorknobs. And if— God forbid—you dared to question her, you were then immediately banished from her little clique, which I aptly titled Barbie Land.

Oh my! Can you imagine such a cruel fate?

Sure, this Barbie had managed to fool some people into doing her bidding. Like blind sheep, the ones who fell for her spell did whatever it took to get in her good graces. To the unperceptive and blind, Barbie had it all in spades: beauty, money, status. She appeared to be the whole package and then some. Therefore, you had to gain her acceptance if you wanted to fit in. These misdirected individuals wished to spend every waking day in Barbie Land, but didn't have the social clearance to do so. And sadly, they never would.

When this Barbie smiled, you were immediately blinded by her disturbingly white teeth. Her fake cheekbones and lips were overly puffy like fresh bee stings. She wanted people to believe that she was a well-versed intellectual, not some Botox-filled pincushion who couldn't stand not getting her way. But like all flimsily built ships, it was only a matter of time until damning leaks would start to show.

When Barbie really wanted something, she would literally ooze with over-the-top sluttiness, complete with fake smiles, playful giggles, cleavage thrusts, and eyelash batting. Donning an inappropriately tight, low-cut dress, she would strut her stuff around the office all day and showcase her supple frame. Attempting to garner the attention of every man in the general vicinity, she would flaunt herself like a raw piece of meat for the jackals to fight over. One by one, they'd get sucked into her trap like flies to an open jar of honey. Now, Barbie oftentimes confused all this fawning for genuine adoration, or a clear sign of her worth and intelligence. Whether that was true or not, they were in fact there to do her bidding.

The Melted Barbie is a breed unto herself, a vindictive and mean species that preys on the sensibilities of horny, shallow men. Around the office, she is the queen of gossip and trash talk. Airing people's dirty laundry is a personal joy of hers, a pastime. Of course, Barbie pretends that she is completely clueless to her obvious indiscretions, but we all know better. The bitch is cunning, to say the least. I'm going out on a limb here, but I feel like her inner dialogue goes a little something like this.

Why should I care about the consequences of my actions? I didn't do anything wrong; I just took advantage of my natural talents. And there ain't nothin' wrong with that, girl. I'm just doin' me. They are the ones who should be ashamed of themselves, slobbering all over me when most of them have wives and children waiting at home. Ugh, men are the worst!

And so on...and so on...

She believes that there is nothing wrong with disposing of people when they are no longer of any use to her. She justifies this heartless act by telling herself that it's okay to recycle acquaintances. That's what they are there for, to simply use up then throw away.

Unfortunately for the Barbie I met, people at the office began to talk and snoop behind her back. One by one, they connected the dots and eventually realized that she was a total fraud. In other words, she was a liar and, in general, a terrible human being. Her exorbitant disposal trends were not of the same caliber as a Louis Vuitton type, though she perceived herself to be. But, an individual of this nature should obviously have morals, good ethics, and respect for others. All things, I might mention, that she did not possess.

To combat this new onslaught of heavy judgment, Barbie defensively surrounded herself with an even bigger entourage of ass-kissers and ass-pinchers alike. She also intentionally insulated her friend group with individuals that were deemed less attractive, especially when compared to her. This ensured that Barbie would always be the prettiest one in the room, and never forced her to question herself. Remember, she needed to always be the centre of attention, no matter the situation. Only once all eyes were on her could she truly feel something akin to happiness.

Ouch.

I'm not sure what caused this severe disconnection from reality. Maybe she inhaled too much hairspray or absorbed too much of the dangerous chemicals in the knockoff bleach she used to strip her hair. My honest impression: she was terribly unhappy with her life choices and the little she had to show for them. In return, she took her frustrations out on everyone else around her instead of facing them head-on. I have since concluded that, in reality, Barbie has a wealth of insecurities that I don't even want to dig into.

Barbie truly believed that if she treated people like servants or second-class citizens, then they would fear and respect her. Not a great plan, but it did seem to work on more than a few. Any face-to-face confrontation caused her great discomfort, so she instead settled all her personal beefs online. With tens of thousands of social media followers to back up every petty argument and dispute, she was practically untouchable. If some sarcastic or rude comment ever graced any of her social media pages, her followers could be weaponized within a matter of hours. They'd use brute force to take down the offender and restore their queen's honour. Much like a self-absorbed toddler who can't see beyond themselves, Barbie saw nothing wrong with how she treated others. To her, it was all well deserved.

I will say that, although Barbie is devoid of emotion, I do pity her now. She is so dense, so inherently naive, that she will never truly understand just what it is that makes her so flawed. Because of this oversight, she will never have a chance to grow as a person. She will never be able to handle the painful truth of who she really is—what she really is. And what is she? Just flesh-toned plastic and straw hair.

Pretty on the outside, but forever hollow on the inside.

Chapter 18
THE TROLL

There is a special type of individual that doesn't fit into any of the previous categories I have listed. This person possesses the ruthless characteristics of a desperado—a real mean bitch who relishes in any and all forms of drama. To call this person a super bitch just isn't accurate enough.

She is...a Troll.

Generally unfriendly and not much in the looks department, the Troll is a cruel individual to her very core. The Troll is also a notorious backstabber, spiteful and bitter just for the sake of it. In her own twisted mind, she is on the same intellectual level as Stephen Hawking or Einstein—a real renaissance woman.

When you first meet the Troll, she is relatively quiet and unassuming, reserved and subtly sophisticated in her own way. But beware; she has an ulterior motive for engaging you. Even before you really get to know the Troll all that well, you will notice that she appears to be well connected and cordial with credible people within the company. You see many of those same people often ask for her advice, only further solidifying the wavering illusion of trust. Unbeknownst to you, the Troll is extremely manipulative and thirsty for validation. But this insatiable hunger will come at a great price to others.

As time progresses, you get to know the Troll on a deeper, more personal level. Slowly, she starts revealing anecdotal stories about other people around the office in an attempt to lull you even further into her trap. In that moment of doubt, you give yourself a mental note to be very careful around this one; she might be trouble. You decide at this point that it would be a good idea to avoid her entirely, bypassing the inevitable drama to come.

Suddenly, you are caught off guard by her constant onslaught of inappropriate commentaries and criticism. And as you gawk at her in utter disbelief, it is apparent that she doesn't sense any of your discomfort. She clearly feels nothing for others—no remorse, no concern. After that unpleasant encounter, you feel increasingly awkward around her and attempt to stop any further attempts at conversation. But, the solution is only temporary.

As time progresses, so does the level of inappropriate banter. Soon, she starts confiding in you about her on-and-off boyfriend. Sorry...cyber boyfriend. In too much detail, she goes on to describe their sexual relationship and kinky taboos. You try to find some redeeming quality in the Troll to make up for such heinous talk, but fail to find so much as a kernel of goodness. This woman has no interest in anything outside of herself; this much is abundantly clear.

The Troll covets all that is not hers. She covets the relationships, possessions, successes and friendships of others. Nothing and no one is safe from her greedy appetites. She clearly doesn't understand that friendship is a reciprocal deal; you get out what you put in. And really, why would anyone want a miserable Troll as their close friend? I know I wouldn't.

And, in the end, her inevitable loneliness will be the final toll to pay.

Chapter 19
THE NARCISSIST

Everyone knows that one guy—and there's always one—who acts like he literally knows everything about everything. So prideful of his vast knowledge of the world, he incessantly boasts about his numerous accomplishments, all of which are fabricated from loose lies he accumulated for show.

This, my friends, is the Narcissist.

He is arrogant and patronizing toward every single person that he encounters. This garish behaviour is amplified by those he perceives to be threats. When approaching these potential challengers, the Narcissist may resort to using an overly condescending tone and a self-righteous attitude to remain on top of the situation.

Naturally, when I met one of these Narcissists in person, I wanted to bitch-slap him upside the head within the first five minutes of hearing him speak. I didn't do it, though. He was an absolute waste of my time and energy. Let's face it; I only have so much time to be passing out much-needed ego checks. And, sadly, I just didn't feel he deserved the lesson from a pro.

Not yet, anyway.

I know it's already implied, but this is one of those individuals that's completely self-centred. I'm talking, like, no empathy whatsoever. In his little mind, his interests take precedence over literally everything and everyone around him. No exception to the rule. As a result, the Narcissist perceives all other human life as merely irrelevant, social collateral to be bartered along the winding path of his own journey. Every moment of every day is happening to and for them, sustaining an ego so large that it has its own gravitational pull.

Fun factoid: the Greek mythical figure Narcissus was a boy who fell in love with his own reflection, and in the spring, he metamorphosed into a flower along the same riverbank. This is where the root of the word "narcissist" derives. I'm sure you already know this, but the thought of how little mankind has changed since those forgotten days of old always makes me chuckle.

The first day that I met this specific Narcissist in question was at my boyfriend's workplace. I was just stopping by to say hello, maybe see if he was free to go out for lunch, when I noticed this mimbo (male bimbo) in the backroom. Facing away from where I stood by the swinging doors, he stared longingly at himself in a full-length mirror while flexing, making sexy faces and taking selfies.

"Oh, look at you, sexy stud," I heard him mumble in a seductive purr, clearly not registering my presence. "What's a smart, handsome devil like yourself doing in a dingy place like this? You should be modeling for Tom Ford runway shows or *Vogue* shoots, not working behind some checkout counter like a slob." At the end of each of these self-administered compliments, the man would twist and stiffen various parts of his body in shaky bodybuilder poses. Trust me; it took everything inside for me not to burst out laughing when I saw this. And just when I thought I heard and saw it all, he swiveled his hips around—ass wiggling back and forth before the smudged mirror—and said, "I don't think there's a lady alive that's good enough for this booty. No, sir. Mm-hmm."

Appalled, yet very intrigued, I stood quietly by the back doors and continued to watch him stroke his inflated ego to the point of combustion. It was fairly obvious that this guy had a wildly distorted image of himself, one that was larger than life and twice as beautiful as reality. From where I was standing, all I saw was a lonely loser who was hugged by their mommy a few too many times and now couldn't see himself for who he really was. It's okay if you aren't a ten on the hotness scale or if you have a mediocre job, but if you have to live in a delusion just to cope with your own shortcomings, then you're just a narcissistic asshole.

And based on what I witnessed firsthand in that back room, I think it's safe to assume that the only person worthy of this guy's attention was his own reflection.

Of course, this was only one of the literally hundreds of mimbos that I've had the pleasure of interacting with. In fact, the one that sticks out the most in my mind to this very day would have to be this vain, shallow manager I had at work a couple years back. I was the supervisor of a telecommunications sales team at the time, overseeing a small crew that worked the phones from morning to night. Like the rest of the crew, I also made sales calls to potential clients. And, not to toot my own horn, but I was pretty damn good at it, too. It was because of these spectacular sales numbers that I was promoted to supervisor in the first place: a much-deserved reward that didn't go unnoticed by my overly vain floor manager, who will remain nameless.

To hell with it; let's call him Ted.

"Come in," Ted said as I slowly opened the shaded door to his office one fateful afternoon. "This won't take long. Close the door and have a seat."

As I was instructed, I stepped inside and shut the door behind me. Hesitantly, I took a seat across from his oversized oak desk. After my promotion to supervisor, he and I hadn't had that much contact throughout the workday. Most times, he would just email me with any random commands or dirty work he needed done, effectively bypassing the usual polite semantics. This avoidant process wasn't ideal, but because I sensed that Ted was a little bit on the entitled side, I let these minor indiscretions go for the sake of workplace comradery. The last thing I wanted to do was make any negative impressions with the stuffy heads in the management pool. But now, we were finally meeting face-to-face for a one-on-one chat. About what exactly, I didn't know, but would soon find out.

"What seems to be the trouble, Ted?" I asked, not liking the grim expression on his glistening, overly lotioned face. I could tell right away, just by looking at the man, that he was extremely vain:

manicured fingernails, expensive tailored suit, slicked-back hair, and plucked eyebrows, among other obvious signs. Regardless, I respected his role as my superior, and assumed he would reciprocate that same respect.

Yeah, I know—wishful thinking on my part. But at the time, I was a little more trusting than I am now.

"Don't take this the wrong way," Ted started to say, skipping all the small talk and getting straight to the marrow of it. "I'm not dragging you in here to discipline you or anything like that. I just wanted to make this absolutely clear right off the bat. Understood?" After I nodded in tentative agreement, he continued, "I need you to do me a personal favor."

Already not liking where this conversation was going, I frowned and replied, "Oh? And what's that?"

Lowering his gaze to his desk, he answered, "I need you to dumb down your sales pitches for this next client call." Coyly, he passed me a call log sheet that contained the client's number and personal information. According to this sheet, the client was listed as having a PhD, among several other academic achievements that were rather impressive. As I read through this detailed list, Ted added, "I know her credentials look legit, but trust me, this lady is a real airhead. Dumber than a sack of hammers."

Offended by such inflammatory talk about a high-profile client, I glanced up from the call sheet at him.

Becoming automatically defensive, he doubled down and said, "She's one of those 'educated idiot' types. Trust me. I've had the displeasure of taking on a sales call with her before. I'd call her myself, but I'm a little too busy to deal with all that."

I noticed a half-finished crossword puzzle sitting out on his desk.

Bullshit, I thought, my anger steadily snowballing into a blizzard inside my head. *You're not busy; you're just too damn smug to do it yourself. You met a woman who's smarter than you and now you can't stand to face her. She challenges that tidy little house of cards you've built up for yourself—the one that takes only one strong wind of actual* mental competence to tear down. And worse, you slander this woman's good name and then expect others to take you seriously as a leader. For shame, Ted. For shame...

At that moment, aside from my annoyed rage, I also felt an unusual pang of sympathy for Ted. It was a known fact around the office that he was going through a messy breakup with his wife of almost twenty years. His co-workers were naturally sympathetic and would try to subtly console him.

"It's all right," he always said, hiding the infinite chasm of sadness deep down. "Sharon was a real bitch. To be honest, I'm just glad it's all over now. I was getting pretty tired of sleeping on the couch every night."

Although these remarks seemed odd to everyone around the office, they all remained supportive during those trying times.

Not even a month after the divorce was finalized, he found "the one."

Ted met this woman at a bar and immediately fell head over heels for her. After the second date, he came into the office ranting and raving to anyone who would listen that he was madly in love and had finally found his true soul mate. He constantly bantered about their fantastic lovemaking, even going so far as to assert that he was her first. How truthful this was, I couldn't say. But judging by her giant fake breasts, ever-present cleavage, and overdone butt injections, I'd guess not.

Before long, the not so cleverly concocted façade started to unravel. Not even two months after meeting, Ted cheated on his soul mate with a much younger stripper, brutally ending the supposedly destined relationship.

This just goes to show—you can't have a soulmate if you never had a soul to begin with.

After many grueling, annoying years of having to encounter this type of deplorable individual over and over again, naturally, I am hungry to find a word or phrase that properly encapsulates their pathetic existence, that simplifies their treacherous lifestyles for any layman to easily divulge. As I started writing this section of critical analysis—a bitch-ignette, if you will—I felt compelled to research the word itself. Narcissist.

Webster's dictionary states that a narcissist is a person that has an inordinate fascination with oneself that often results in excessive self-love and vanity. This vague description led me to the psychoanalytical definition of the word provided by dictornary.com, which states that a narcissist is a person that "derives erotic gratification from admiration of one's own physical or mental attributes, being a normal condition at the infantile level of personality development."

My theory on the whole thing is that people of this mindset have an uncontrollable need to be admired and/or revered by literally everyone around them. It's more about how other people perceive them than who they actually are as a person. To them, a decent front—no matter how phony or ill-conceived it may be—is totally necessary for daily life. Some would even find these strenuous efforts to hide their true selves to be somewhat commendable. Think of all the trouble they went through just to convince the world that they're someone they're not. Every waking moment must be dedicated to keeping the illusion alive, or else they will face almost certain persecution. I think we can all agree that this wouldn't be an easy feat for any of us.

Yet, I look at this behaviour and can't help but wonder if the problem goes a little deeper than just a concern for outer appearances. When you clear away the manipulative smoke screen and remove the trick mirrors from their gated personalities, you often find that these people are desperately insecure, plagued by insurmountable feelings of inadequacy and dangerously low self-worth. The Narcissist constantly craves attention, whether it be positive or negative. They will even go as far as to pay top dollar for it. Their obvious ineptitude in maintaining any resemblance of a social connection or meaningful relationship is unavoidably sad. Sad, but tragically real.

For the Narcissist, the internal struggle never ends.

Chapter 20
THE FAKE FRIEND

We all have people who we consider to be close acquaintances and trusted friends, their worth wholly determined by their individual actions and influences on our lives. And, as you might know, the cruel hands of fate never hesitate to throw more challenging curveballs at you over the passing years. Because of this constant grind, some, who you once considered to be close confidants, fade away. Like spectral apparitions, they slowly disappear from your inner circle and are forgotten. Why is this?

Well, to put it simply, they just don't get you as a person anymore. You've outgrown them, husking their company like a snake sheds a layer of dead skin. Out with the old, in with the new. But don't feel bad about this involuntary action. These fair-weather friends are fickle, not to mention faker than a three dollar bill.

Here are two examples of those types of "friends" that I have been forced to endure.

Dawna and I met while we were both attending university. Since the inception of our friendship, I had never once seen her not actively involved in a romantic relationship. Truly, Dawna couldn't stand to be without a partner to claim as her own. I jokingly labelled her the "serial dater" due to the sheer number of boyfriends she had accumulated over the years. With Dawna, it was never about the quality of her men, but the fact that they were physically there with her. I used to frequently kid that if a guy had a pulse, Dawna would date him. When she broke up with one boyfriend, another one was right in line, waiting for his turn up at bat.

All of this would've been fine with me—hey, it's her life, not mine—if she wasn't always trying to act like each new random guy was her future husband. The guys she dated were deadbeats, dropouts and has-beens with nothing to offer but empty promises. As her close friend at the time, I knew that any infusion of reality or truth regarding this endless onslaught of boyfriends would instantly make me out to be an undermining bitch. Despite this, I came dangerously close on several occasions to just asking her why she was so desperate not to be alone.

Is she so brainwashed by society that she believes she was made incomplete and entirely insignificant without a man by her side? What the hell happened to being liberated, being independent and free of the patriarchy?

And for a long time, I kept these questions tucked safely away inside my head. One day, I just couldn't stand to keep them locked up any longer.

Dawna and I always had a Christmas/New Year's dinner where we would go to a decadent restaurant and consume a hearty meal, which was later followed by a calorie-induced coma back at our dorm room. But on the last holiday celebration we planned together, she had rescheduled and changed the date so many times that I honestly lost count. And soon, I found out the reason why I had been getting blown off for weeks on end. Dawna kept postponing our dinner to instead hang out with whatever man she was with on that given day. Completely infatuated, she chose their sloppy company over our supposedly solid friendship.

Upset by the discovery, I forced Dawna to sit down and seriously question our friendship. Here I was, always making adjustments in my personal schedule to accommodate for her wants and needs, listening for hours while she bitched and moaned about all her romantic woes. And for what? Just to get stabbed in the back and betrayed, I guess.

Upon much reflection, I quickly determined that Dawna was transforming into a thoughtless and self-absorbed person: a Fake Friend. Clearly, her only priority in life was to chase men. I was a mere stage prop to her now, that friend she picked up and used when things weren't going exactly her way. Soon after this dire realization, I broke off our friendship for good.

To be brutally honest, there was never any spilled milk on my end.

This leads us to the second type of friend. Her name was Nahla, and she was a devoted friend at one time in my life—someone who, in my eyes, could do no wrong. Admittedly, I relied on her for sound advice, guidance, and overall companionship throughout the years. Not to understate this, but I told Nahla EVERYTHING. My thoughts, feelings, opinions—she was like my personal therapist and homegirl all rolled up into one beautiful person. Foolishly, I thought we had a sacred trust, an unbreakable bond, but I was terribly mistaken. Little did I know that Nahla was secretly on a mission to further herself at any expense to others, including your humble narrator.

But whenever I started to make the painful transition of branching away from her to make other friends, she always found a way to involve herself. This Fake Friend was so terribly insecure that she invented a complex web of lies to keep my waning attention (mysterious illnesses, personal rumours that had no basis in fact, etc.). A little wiser this time around, I knew that all these tales were just elaborate fabrications designed to titillate my curiosity and pull at my heartstrings. A small part of me wanted to believe that at one time Nahla had good intentions, but maybe became just a little misguided along the way. All positive assumptions aside, I knew in my heart of hearts that this was just a symptom of being too trusting of a person. I wanted so badly to believe that Nahla wanted only the best for me, but my perceived wants and hopes would not change a damn thing. Really, she was more like a wolf in sheep's clothing than the friend I so desperately wanted to keep.

But then, completely out of the blue, Nahla began taking liberties with our already fragile friendship. She started asking to borrow money and secretly made obnoxious comments to my inner circle of friends about me when I wasn't around. This was the final straw that broke the camel's back.

Gradually, I started learning of all the angst and drama she had caused in and around my peer group. I remember being so hurt and thinking, *How could Nahla do his to me after all that I've done for her? What drove her to do me in like this? Seriously, I've spent so many sleepless nights comforting her and loaning her money when she needed it, not to mention putting up with her slutty antics.*

On top of all that, I also helped Nahla find an apartment after graduation. I assembled furniture with a butter knife at two in the damn morning and emotionally supported her when she was at odds with her family. Through thick and thin, I was always there by her side when she needed me, like any good friend would be.

And after all that self-sacrifice, this was the thanks I got? Yeah... thanks, but no thanks. I could seriously do without all that bull mess.

When I made the plan to finally sever our ties, I decided that if she owned up to her shortcomings, I might forgive her. Maybe. But she immediately got defensive and started arguing with me about trivial things that I knew to be true. Rather quickly, I got irritated with hearing her half-assed excuses and spoke up.

"You know what, Nahla?" I said, my voice even and calm despite the anger bubbling under my skin. "You are one seriously tormented bitch with severe self-doubt issues. As of this moment, I am done with you and your craziness. I want you to respect my privacy and give me some much-needed space. Can you do that?"

Short answer: she could not.

Immediately after I hung up with her, she called everyone I knew and stirred up another shitstorm of rumours and false accusations about me. Then came the personal attacks. I was literally stunned by the vicious attitude Nahla exhibited in all the nasty calls, emails and texts that I got from her in the following weeks. But, even through all that nonsense, I knew that I did the right thing in the end.

To quote an old friend of mine who didn't stab me in the back, "If the bitch ain't your friend, then she's deadweight, honey. Best to just toss her ass overboard and keep on sailin'."

And really, who the hell could disagree with that sound piece of logic?

Chapter 21
THE CYCLOPS

When I was young, my mother would force me to endure afternoon tea with her, her friend Francine, and Francine's unbelievably annoying daughter, Sue. I would fight tooth and nail to avoid these awkward meetings. Sometimes I could wriggle my way out of it with white lies involving extra homework or chores to finish, but most times, I had no choice. Despite my best efforts, I spent countless hours of my teenage years sipping tea and listening to the most innate gossip known to mankind.

Francine was one of those desperately cheerful people that, in reality, had an intensely dull and trifling life. She would look for any way to add a glimmer of meaning or validation to her existence, and would often use her ugly daughter as a catalyst. She would even go as far as to share multiple stories of how wonderful and flawless Sue was: the perfect daughter and student. And to further punch this faulty point home, Francine would justify her weird opinions by drawing unsubstantiated parallels between Sue and me. Sue was the shining example of budding success, and I was...well...the opposite. Although she would never come outright and say it, Francine saw me as a loser, a social leper that would simply float through life and never achieve anything worthy of praise or admiration.

Long story short, Francine didn't think too highly of me.

"You oughta see that she gets a good education," Francine often told my mother during our forced get-togethers, all while I sat not even two feet away. "Make sure she gets a real job someday. If she's lucky, that is..." Before my mom could politely protest such an assuming remark, Francine continued, "Don't get me wrong. Your daughter's a lovely girl, but she's nothing more than a dreamer. Her head is always stuck in the clouds." Right on cue, the comparisons started. "Look at Sue; she already has a postsecondary education and a wonderful career path ahead of her. Now, there's someone that has big things lined up for them in the future. Yes, big things, indeed."

As much as I wanted to bite that old bitty's head off for speaking so rudely to my own mother, I wasn't about to give Francine more ammunition to slander me with around town. Did she really think I was stupid enough to fall for such a blatant trap? Well...probably. But despite her less than ideal opinions of me, I was not completely clueless as to her intentions.

The years passed and I went off to attend university, earning both an undergraduate and graduate degree along the way. It had been a while, but eventually, that crusty old bitch would reappear. Like a bad case of herpes, I knew it was only a matter of time until Francine showed up unannounced to ruin my whole day. And sure enough, it happened one cloudy afternoon while I was visiting home for the weekend.

I was walking around the block, trying to get in some cardio, when I saw her. Passing by her front yard, I pretended not to see her taking the trash out to the curb. As I quickened my pace—eyes cast down to the cracked pavement—I prayed she wouldn't recognize me and would just go back inside her house without incident. But as I tried my hardest to look nonchalant and to keep cruising, it happened.

"Vivienne! Hey! Over here!" Waving both her hands wildly over her head to get my attention, Francine hurriedly crossed the street and approached me with open arms. "Hey, you!" she cooed, wrapping her arms around my shoulders for a big fake hug and trapping me in place. "How're you?! You're looking well. How's school going? I heard from your mom that you were having a bit of trouble last semester." Before I could shut down the false idea, she quickly added, "Oh, I know. You should come by my place later for some tea, just like old times! Wouldn't that be great? Sue won't be able to stop by, but we can still catch up. You remember Sue, don't you? My, she's really something. Why, just the other day she called and told me the most wonderful story about her trip to—"

Cutting the head off the snake before the verbal venom could sink into my bruised ego, I interjected, "Okay, okay, I'll stop by for some tea later."

With that, I ended the conversation and went on my way. I knew my promise would be upheld, lest I face the wrath of my mother for bailing. There was no doubt in my mind that Francine would rat me out in a heartbeat, resulting in a shameful browbeating from *Mommie Dearest*. It's funny, but even now I'd still do almost anything to avoid disappointing my mother.

All too soon, the time came to wander over to Francine's place. Before I could even get my jacket off in the extremely small foyer of her cottage-style home, she swiftly launched onto the topic of Sue.

"She just completed university with a BSW and now works for the government as a social worker," Francine blathered on as she ushered me to the kitchen. "Blissfully married, too—he's a brain surgeon. Very sweet and loving man, and he's paid well, too. Makes more money than the two know what to do with, really."

As I politely digested this load of informational bullshit, I saw it. On the way to the kitchen, at the end of a short hallway, was a literal shrine devoted to Sue. Carefully pasted in a neat collage on the wall were individual snapshots of her life, and the strange display was lit by the flame of a single candle. Right away, a chill ran down my spine like the march of a thousand baby spiders across my exposed skin.

Noticing my puzzled stare, Francine stopped and commented, "Isn't it beautiful? God, she grew up so fast. It's just amazing how far she's come. Honestly, I couldn't be prouder of Sue; she's more than any mother could ever ask for in a daughter."

The impulse to vomit in my mouth was intense. In case some of you don't know, this is not normal behaviour for any mother to display. In fact, I would consider this oddly obsessive, even cultish. Either way, I was seriously creeped out by the whole scene.

Entering the kitchen, Francine sat me down at the dinner table and continued to tell me about Sue's outstanding accomplishments since childhood. Mindlessly jabbering for minutes on end, Francine finally stopped bragging long enough to ask me, "So, are you attending any sort of postsecondary schools? Sue did, and passed with flying colours. No surprise there, though. She's always been an overachiever."

Smiling, I did my best to keep any sort of spite out of my voice and replied, "I actually completed both an undergraduate and graduate degree from two prestigious universities. Didn't my mother tell you any of this already?"

An expression of forced remembrance dawned upon her wrinkled face, and then Francine smirked and said, "Perhaps, but I can't remember. Oh, Sue's degree is an important one, too. It's one of those three-year types for people who want to lead in their fields. And, as you know, anyone lucky enough to have an honours degree is just waiting for the money to roll in. Well, one thing is for sure; an exceptionally talented young woman like Sue won't have to wait long."

Even now, I'm not sure why she felt the need to waste so much breath on such pointless talking points. In retrospect, I just can't see how she would think I'd be interested in hearing her trivial stories about someone I hadn't even spoken to since high school. The only reason that comes to mind is that Francine was only telling me these things to make me feel bad. To further solidify this vague assumption, she went on to brag about Sue's wonderous life for what felt like hours, never once stopping to allow me a chance to chime in. Not that I'd have had anything civil to say.

The inhumane torture finally stopped when Francine paused her rant to get some more tea and cookies. When she was out of earshot on the other side of the kitchen, I took a deep breath and quietly uttered, "Serenity now...serenity now..."

I remember wishing so badly that Elaine, Jerry, Kramer, George or even Newman were there to guide me through this living hell. But little did I know, the hurting had only just begun.

When Francine came back to the table, she had more than just extra cookies. Laid out in front of me were the dreaded frilly wrappings of a wedding album. Sue's wedding album, to be precise.

Page after page, I had to bite my lip and pretend to be impressed by such an atrociously garish ceremony. Now, I should say that, even in her youth, Sue would never be described as a pageant queen. But those pictures—her lumpy frame stuffed into an oversized wedding gown—made her look like a dressed-up bag of potatoes. I don't mean to be rude, just honest. The fact that someone with working eyesight would willingly marry someone so unattractive was a testament to the complexities of love. Lazy left eye still on prominent display, Sue looked cross-eyed in every single picture. Her head appeared large and loomed like a Cyclops, and even with this supposedly advanced salary of hers, I saw that Sue's fashion sense hadn't improved much over the years. Upon further inspection, the wedding dress was clearly used: a last-minute Goodwill find if I ever saw one.

And, girl, don't even get me started on how schlubby her new husband looked. That's a whole other can of worms entirely.

In the end, I was glad I had tea with Francine one last time. The closure was well worth the hassle.

Chapter 22
THE MEAN BITCH

Now seems like a good time to do a quick overview of what we've covered.

Thus far, I've written vignettes about Melted Barbies, Trolls, the Cyclops, Crazy Bitch Bosses, and so much more. With all that in mind, I decided that this book wouldn't be complete without exposing one last common social archetype.

I present to you, the Mean Bitch.

Simply put, the Mean Bitch is your worst nightmare. She is pretentious, bitter, spoiled, shallow, manipulative, controlling, insecure, vindictive, and pretty much every other nasty adjective you can think of. When the Mean Bitch first enters your life, her false faces and cheerful veil seem great at first, and her carefree demeanor appears genuine. But things aren't always as they initially appear. As soon as she establishes a line of mutual trust, the Mean Bitch will immediately offer to help you in any possible way. Be warned, because her good graces come at great detriment to your well-being.

The Mean Bitch is only interested in helping others if she can benefit tenfold in return. As you get to know her better, you will discover that she is not very well liked by most of your other friends. They can't stand her or her phony ways. They will secretly complain about her fake laughter, constant showboating, and general obnoxiousness. But in the mind of a Mean Bitch, she is the paragon of virtue. She sits alone on the throne of ultimate judgment, and everyone else is merely a faceless simpleton by comparison. The unfortunate side effect of succumbing to these grandiose delusions is that she never engages in self-reflective practices and, in turn, never fully realizes the vastness of her own shortcomings. She never judges herself with the same standards and rules she uses to judge others, and the Mean Bitch encompasses the mindset of a compulsive liar.

Outwardly beautiful, but ignorantly flawed.

The Mean Bitch thinks that she can have whatever she wants, exactly when she wants it.

When she was a little girl, she would run to Daddy and have all her desires met without question. All she had to do was put on a dour expression, bat her long eyelashes a few times, and Daddy would handle the rest. This spawned a spoiled mentality that only festered like an old hunk of cheese over the years. Like most stubborn children, the Mean Bitch cannot accept "no" for an answer.

She compares herself to others who have accomplished so much more than she ever will. But does she look at them and find inspiration or drive in their successful endeavours? No. Quite the opposite, actually. The Mean Bitch just complains that she could do great things, too, if everyone around her weren't holding her back. How any of this makes sense is anyone's guess. Regardless of the truth, she will get irrationally angry if someone much more qualified than her gets in her way. Let's use a failed job interview as an example. This inevitably leads to one of her epic meltdowns, which brings her friend group into a downward spiral with her. In her mind, that reward belonged to her—period. Her internal monologue in the face of all of this probably sounds something like this.

What makes that old bitch so special? She's not better than me; no one is. They probably only gave her the job over me because they felt bad for her. Oh well, her trashy ass probably did things I'm not willing to do. Nasty!

I know, I know. If you're anything like me, your first reaction to this would be to tell her that she's acting like a spoiled little brat. The woman in question had an MBA from Harvard, something that the Mean Bitch would never attain. Perhaps if she had any kind of degree, then finding a job wouldn't be such a grueling challenge for her. You want to say all this, but you don't.

It just ain't worth the trouble.

Obviously, the Mean Bitch has a great sense of entitlement and instantly becomes upset when her friends sport the latest Burberry trench or Vuitton purse that she has yet to purchase. She will not hesitate to display her true colours by stating at least one of the following jabs:

a) The product in question is a cheap knockoff.
b) It's real, but not new, and the fact that it was purchased secondhand brings down the item's worth.

This gut reaction almost always stems from intense jealousy, and is rarely contained for the sake of politeness. I recall one occasion when a group of my old friends got together for drinks. Off the cuff, one of them asked the group if anyone had ever travelled outside of North America. Before anyone could answer, the Mean Bitch stole the spotlight.

"Oh yeah," she cooed, overly proud of the long-winded story she was about to tell. "I just took a trip to Zurich not even a year ago. Guys, it was two weeks of unsurpassed luxury; the hotel I stayed at was five-star. By far the classiest place I've ever seen in my whole life. You should all really visit sometime if you can."

Except for the part about visiting Zurich, I knew it was all a lie.

I know exactly where she stayed; she showed me the hotel's shabby website while booking the trip. It wasn't a five-star resort as she had claimed. Hell, it was not even a four- or three-star. In reality, it was a total cracker box. But, due to the affordable rates, she decided it would be best to book there. Following in this tradition of thriftiness, she also paid for her flight using air miles she'd saved up. Even her tickets to the adjacent ski resort were free of charge.

I know this because I had generously given her the exclusive ski pass as a belated birthday gift.

The Mean Bitch expects everyone to bow down to her and kiss her feet. Varying opinions are fine, as long as they don't directly conflict with her fragile viewpoints. Threatening to contact the police under the guise of filing ridiculous lawsuits against you is a common defense mechanism for her when challenged. Of course, she will always spew hateful slurs in a juvenile attempt to cut you down to size; that's just normal for her.

Based on the dignified way that she carries herself, you would think the Mean Bitch was a former pageant queen pageant winner—someone who used to be famous but had since fallen from grace. The Mean Bitch strategically chooses to surround herself with the most insecure and weak people. They pose the least amount of danger, and their blind obedience to her emotional tyranny is all but ensured. Each one is nothing more than a faceless cog in the machine, a disposable part to be used and then promptly thrown away.

In true Mean Bitch fashion, she will not think twice about posting glamorously edited pictures of herself on Instagram for everyone to admire. However, if you dare post an unflattering picture of her, she will lose her mind and send a barrage of threatening texts until it's taken down. She will also post cryptic status updates and moody comments on other people's social media feeds to keep the attention on her. More than anything, she can't stand seeing others garner more attention than her. Whether it's news of a couple's blissful marriage, or a terrible cancer diagnosis shared amongst grieving families and friends, all eyes and minds must always rest upon her beautiful face.

She may be the Mean Bitch, but she sure as hell isn't a smart one. That's for sure.

Chapter 23
BRIDEZILLA

When some girls are growing up, their parents, relatives, and society at large try to decide their fates. It is unanimously decided that the girl's destiny is to someday meet that special someone, settle down in a committed relationship, and bear children. This lifelong commitment will ensure that this once helpless little girl takes the last big step toward inner fulfillment. Now a grown woman, the entire trajectory of her budding life is focused on acquiring one sacred object.

The wedding ring.

It should be noted that this is no ordinary ring that I speak of, but one of epic proportions. It must possess a certain "bling" or "sparkle" factor, and both the colour and the cut should be the fanciest ones available on the free market. The idea is already programmed in her vulnerable brain that it must be the type of ring that could stab all her close friends with venomous envy. Once the ring is acquired, the bride-to-be slowly moves toward the uncharted waters of prenuptial affairs. For her, there is much planning to be done for that big day, that holy union of the decade. During the process of formulating a picture-perfect wedding, a drastic change occurs.

This is her metamorphosis into the dreaded Bridezilla.

For her, this would be the wedding to end all weddings, a garish affair that everyone would be talking about for years to come. I'm not sure if it's self-inflicted stress that forces the bride to self-actualize, but the transformation is practically unstoppable once initiated. Regardless, weddings seem to bring out the worst attributes in her, which then cause everyone to cringe.

And cringe they shall.

This extreme display of mental fragility was clearly demonstrated in the case of my good friend Dianne. Dianne was a relatively calm and stable person, but when her long-time boyfriend, Marco, proposed, all hell broke loose. Like a dictator, she forced everyone that might be even remotely involved in her wedding (minus the groom, his family, and friends) to view EVERY single wedding dress she thought about buying. I must have looked at over one hundred dresses that she just didn't find to be suitable. She finally settled on a custom couture creation from Galia Lahav.

As a friend, I was also expected to donate every waking moment of my life helping her plan for the big day. Needless to say, by the third week of planning, I was completely exhausted from both that and the grind of work. I was required at all times to be cheerful, supportive and kind, even when she went off the rails and threw a tantrum for one stupid reason or another. Bridezilla can't stand to be told when she's acting like a spoiled brat and isn't thinking rationally; this only fuels the outrage. At the drop of a dime, she would become wildly defensive and emotional. I had to suffer through the endless discussions over tablecloth patterns, stylized napkins, elaborate centrepieces, and flower bouquets. With a mandatory phony smile, I internally justified her selfish behaviour as nothing more than a case of temporary insanity from the various pressures involved in making such a huge life decision.

Unfortunately, the madness didn't stop there.

As the wedding day loomed closer and closer, we were all on high alert. The task of damage control wasn't mentioned in the invitation, but was an unspoken duty of any who had been appointed a bridesmaid, such as myself. As predicted, the wedding ceremony went off without a hitch. Against the odds, Dianne walked down the aisle looking absolutely stunning in her flowing white dress. At the reception that followed, she had some time to absorb and reflect upon all that had happened to her in the past several months of planning. Dianne came to realize that she hadn't painted a very pretty picture of herself amongst her friends, and selfishness was replaced by guilt.

"I'm so sorry, you guys," Dianne cried apologetically at the bridesmaids' table during the reception. "I've been acting like a total diva this whole time and I only now just realized it. Ugh, I feel so terrible. Can you gals ever forgive me?"

Knowing then in my heart that this apology was completely authentic, I rose from my chair and gave a weepy Dianne a hug. "Of course we do," I said earnestly for the whole group while wrapped up in her friendly embrace. "It's all right; we all know how stressful these things can be." Riding the momentum of the moment, I jokingly added, "But yeah, you've been a major bitch about this whole wedding. Seriously, don't ever ask me to do this for you ever again."

Taking the slighted comment with poise, Dianne offered me a kind smile in return. "I don't blame you for saying that. But, if this all ends well, I won't have to have another wedding, right?!"

At that, the entire table broke out into a fit of unhinged laughter—together once again.

I guess I was wrong; sometimes a Bridezilla can come back from the dark side.

No joke, but there are also Bridezillas who live in trailer parks! As shocking as it may seem, this version is just as irritating as the regular Bridezilla, but possibly twice as deadly. She feels entitled to a blinged-out wedding even though the funds were never there for such an ostentatious occasion. When she mentions to people that she longs for a Lane diamond to put on her finger, I suspect she might be referring to Neil Lane.

"I want that famous Asian lady to design my wedding dress," she'll ignorantly boast while in the company of her trashy friends. "Ya know...that lady with the funny name...what is it? Vera Wang, I think."

After binge watching too much *Entertainment Tonight*, her

real-life expectations are way off the charts. Never that bright of a bulb to begin with, Trailer Park Bridezilla will stubbornly set out on a mission to raise funds for her ill-fated union. The services she provides, I care not to mention.

One word: gross.

Soon, the countdown begins to the Trailer Park Bridezilla's big day; she's even sent out a dedicated status on Facebook reminding all those unfortunate friends of hers of the date. She tells her guests to dress appropriately for the occasion, which means sandals and cargo shorts for the guys, booty shorts and plunging V-necks for the ladies. The wedding reception is held at a musty old Elks Lodge with tacky drugstore decorations, terribly overcooked barbecue, and of course, the final piece to any white trash wedding.

The cash bar.

I suppose some women do become deranged during bridal festivities, but one truth remains. Finally, to all of you normal people out there: hope and pray that you are never asked to participate in a friend's wedding.

For if you do, it might cost you a lot more than just your sanity.

Chapter 24
THE ENTITLED ONES

I love millennials. I really do. One of my nearest and dearest friends, Jill, is of that futuristically named generation. Truth be told, I simply adore Jill—her vigor, confidence, and strong sense of community are all admirable traits. We first met at work, where she was known around the office as the tech queen. She was a whiz when it came to anything computer-related, a skill that I still seriously lack. Jill also became the office aficionado on identifying anything that was worthy of its own Instagram hashtag. More than anything, she wanted to be internet famous.

Inherently entitled, she thought that after putting in six months at a job, she was automatically deserving of a senior manager position. Now, Jill was a good worker and all, but not very punctual or self-driven enough to land such a lofty promotion. But those reasonable facts didn't sit right with Jill.

"If I've said it once, I've said it a thousand times," she ranted to me one day in the company breakroom. "Women deserve monthly days off for PMS! I mean, like, plastic surgery, Botox, fillers, and liposuction should all be covered under the company benefits plan. Why not periods too?"

Now, as a forty-something senior leader in the organization and Jill's self-appointed mentor, I could only roll my eyes in response to such an ill-informed comment. I asked her, "And what if they did offer coverage for periods? What then? Would you want to get paid days off every time you felt constipated or sad? Or maybe we should all just get paid to sit at home and scroll mindlessly through Facebook until our eyeballs fall out. Seriously, where does it end?"

After earnestly contemplating my sarcastic proposal, Jill bobbed her pretty little head before confidently responding, "Well...I don't get constipated. But that other stuff sounds pretty cool."

Lowering my head in shame, I thought, *Kid, your brain is constipated. And may God help us if you're ever put in a position where that same brain has to be held accountable for something.*

Although this chapter isn't about one specific person, I thought it ought to stay in the "people" section of this book!

Chapter 25
PLASTICALLY PERFECT

When I was younger, I couldn't understand why other girls my age wanted so desperately to look older and sexier than they were. But before I knew it, I hit my late thirties and forties. Suddenly, the struggle to retain physical beauty became a vital necessity. Every day I looked in the mirror to find more bags under my eyes, unsightly marionette lines in my skin, deflated lips—just to name a few signs that I was in fact getting older. This frightful realization was all I needed to introduce myself to the wide world of Botox.

Initially, I was more than a little skeptical about joining the ranks of middle-aged women injecting Botox and fillers strategically into their faces. Luckily, I had an experienced friend, Rachel, who convinced me that it was the only logical step to take.

"It's so easy!" she'd boast proudly, showing off her abnormally puffy lips and raised cheekbones. "You should come with me to my next lip appointment and get something done! It takes about forty-five minutes, and you'll look absolutely stunning afterward. I promise."

Grudgingly, I agreed to go. And honestly, I was surprised to discover that my first experience went extremely well. Soon after viewing the immediate uplift and smoothing that the injections did for my aging face, I was hooked. Like an Amish kid in a candy store, I saw the wonderful new world of plastic surgery as my one-way ticket back to physical perfection. But for most of my friends, my sudden desire to achieve plastic perfection was incredibly disturbing.

Ganging up on me every chance they got, they'd take turns

spitting discouraging remarks like, "You don't need to go through all this, Viv! You should just accept the process like the rest of us and age gracefully. What's the point of chasing standards that you'll never reach? It's borderline crazy!"

So, without the safety net of my close friends, I persistently forged ahead on my plastic adventure—alone, but not perturbed in the slightest.

I quickly learned that not all injectors are created equal. Trust me, Botox and lip fillers are particularly painful for those of us who don't like needles. Strangely enough, though, the best people to administer injections aren't the plastic surgeons, but the nurses. Through trials and tribulations, I learned that great lips are not made in a day, but rather sculpted and contoured with precision and patience by an artiste (aka the injector). Little tip: Friday is the worst day to visit a sketchy clinic for cheap work because they are usually pushing the shitty stuff that needs to go before the expiration date. But, as always, buyer beware.

Now, as you can probably tell by that last admission, I've had more than my fair share of bad plastic surgery experiences. It took me six years of getting injections full of lumpy fillers that overinflated my lips, making me look like a duck. I personally despise when people claim that they only get plastic surgery so they can look normal again—like their old selves, but better. First off, I'm admittedly ninety-eight percent fake, and I love being plastically perfect. Let's just get that out there now.

Botched boobs and buttocks are painful, by the way. Not to keep pointing out the obvious, but plastic surgery is not for the faint of heart. Even something as simple as getting your lips done can really hurt like a son of a bitch. Some surgeries are so painful that they'll leave you in a Percocet-induced paradise for days on end. The swelling and bruising leave you looking like you just lost six rounds in the ring against Mike Tyson. These unwanted physical side effects can last for weeks, sometimes months. I've learned that you look downright awful long before you start to retain any amount of fake beauty. Like sculpting a living statue of flesh, bone and cartilage, it's a very long process.

By far, the easiest cosmetic surgery is a facelift, and the most painful is a Brazilian butt lift. Who knew that sitting on your ass could be so painful? The nurses at the private facility that did mine weren't interested in hearing me whine about the amount of pain I was in, though. The only place I could properly air my grievances was a plastic surgery forum online.

For me, the worst part of cosmetic surgery has to be getting the damn IV in. I honestly don't understand how the anesthesiologist doesn't know how to start an IV, and instead treats the inside of my arm like a damn pincushion. After about half a dozen stabs, they finally manage to find a worthy vein to spike. I must admit that the restful sleep that follows is by far the best part of the whole ordeal.

Of course, people always judge me and my plastically perfect adventures. My response to that kind of negative criticism is plain and simple; it's my money, my body, and my choice. I don't seek validation or approval for my recent physical modifications. I didn't do this for anyone else but me. If you don't want modifications, that's your choice. I don't judge you, so pretty please don't judge me. There's no need to shame me by calling me vain or superficial.

I once had a boyfriend that felt the need to call a therapist and try to set up an intervention to help me with my "plastic surgery addiction." I guess getting a breast lift and implants equals mental instability. Funny, I didn't hear him complaining about it when we were in bed together. Between groping and massaging my new parts, he could barely say my name, let alone complain.

Really, plastic surgery is one of the greatest human inventions to ever grace God's green earth—if used in moderation, that is. If taken too far, it can become highly addictive and sometimes fatal. My advice to anyone looking to get some work done would be to pick your surgeon wisely and not skimp.

Believe me; the unhealable scars just aren't worth the few extra pennies you save.

Random Things That Are Just Plain Irritating

Chapter 26

WTF, FACEBOOK AND INSTAGRAM?

Even though I am of the older ilk, I must confess that I consider myself to be a regular user of social media. My favourite of the lot being the notoriously popular Facebook. From time to time, I'll post a cute picture, update my status to reflect something of significance that may be occurring in my life, or vent about random annoyances. You know, the regular stuff that everybody mindlessly posts.

I think Facebook and Instagram are a great way to connect with friends that live all across the globe, and to reconnect with people who were an important part of your formative years but with whom you've since lost touch. There are some people that just don't care much for social media, and I get that, too. But what I don't get are those people over the age of fifteen that post every five minutes or so, clogging up my feed with their pointless memes and unimportant updates that no one cares to hear about. I am not sure if they are even aware that they're so despised amongst other users. This is due in part to the fact that most people are just too nice to say anything.

I once joined a public Facebook group, hoping to share my opinions, sentiments and disdain with other like-minded people. But anytime I posted my thoughts in the group, some thin-skinned dweeb would jump on it and rudely tell me to, "Shut the hell up."

To that witty response, I always said something along the lines of, "If I did that, then you'd have no reason to leave your mom's basement."

To further demonstrate people's inability to grasp the painfully obvious, I want to discuss the seemingly innocent act of posting pictures of your children on Facebook and Instagram. For instance, many of my cohorts on Facebook and Instagram have settled down and chosen to reproduce. I understand that, to many people, having children is nothing short of a blessing from God. As new parents, they are bursting with pride and want to capture and share all those precious memories to post on social media. Candid pictures and video clips of their mushy offspring soon flood everyone's feeds, literally clogging up the works. But sweet Jesus, Mary and Joseph, do I really need to see five hundred plus pictures of your kids sleeping or sucking on a pacifier? Does anyone? It just seems excessive, is all. Don't get me wrong. I'm glad that you're so proud of your child and want to share it with the world, but the last time that I checked, Facebook and Instagram weren't holding any casting calls for future Disney or Nickelodeon stars. I know that it's probably difficult for people to hear this, but your kids are just not that cute.

Sorry, not sorry.

Another hated online personality trope commonly found on Facebook and Instagram is the digital slut. These are the men and women who take highly suggestive photos and videos of themselves and post them for everyone and their mother to peep at. Personally, I don't need to know what the sexy lingerie that your man bought you looks like, or what your plans are for it later that night. I know that you two are in the blessed honeymoon stage of your relationship, but no one cares.

I also can't fathom those people who have a need to relentlessly attack each other online. I get that we all have differences, and sometimes those differences lead to conflict, but this kind of psychological warfare is getting out of hand.

Take, for example, the timeless tale of the jaded lovers.

Broken up and on bad terms, the former couple goes about airing out all of their dirty laundry for everyone to see. They wage war against each other, slinging inappropriate words in message threads and captioned photos that have nothing to do with them. I suppose attacking one another over the computer makes the confrontation seem a little less real, maybe even trivial and almost fun. But it's apparent to anyone with more than two active brain cells that all they're doing is trying to establish teams amongst their shared friend groups. Systematically, the lines will be drawn in the sand, each friend breaking off from the rest depending on which side they decide to take.

For the broken couple, the battle of their doomed relationship might be over, but the vindictive competition against each other has only just begun.

And then there are those individuals that somehow manage to "find" you on Facebook and Instagram. Always by happenstance, I might add; I have a theory that these same lonely saps must spend hours trolling and lurking online in an attempt to make some new friends. And if they aren't looking for friends, then they are just being digital peepers. Obviously, I'm using the term "friends" very loosely here.

But you want to know what the scariest part of all that mess is? This pathetic collection of sketchy social media stalkers could be literally anybody. I repeat, ANYBODY! It could be someone you work with using a convincing alias to trick you, or even some creepazoid with a hacked account pretending to be someone you know and trust in real life. Please, take my advice and just steer clear of uploading your entire friends list to social media. I know it's a lot more convenient than the little black book from back in my day, but trust me, honey, it just ain't worth all the glaring risks. When you put your entire persona online, you're inviting every greasy weirdo to come along and hijack your personal information. Or worse...

Plus, no one likes those wannabe hashtag warriors. Just...ew. Next, please.

However, this solitary rule of self-realization comes at a great cost to your own social group. For when you break from the activities of a generation, you risk being isolated and/or annoyed for your deviance.

"How come you didn't accept my friend request? Huh?" they will ask you, pride and feelings clearly hurt by your very logical and necessary precautions. Sure, you can try to play the disconnected card and claim that you don't go online much and hadn't noticed their request. But it's never enough. Trying to spare the feelings of your nearest and dearest friends—who only want you to be inclusive with them on all viable platforms—you stall the social obligation and promise to add them later. Granted, this will buy you a little more time, but only a couple of days or so. Really, not much. Eventually, they will start pestering you all over again, and this time with a lot more guilt.

And then, after having to hear the same petty questions over and over again, you cave and press the accept button. You put up your best fight, but the popular opinion wins out in the end. Don't beat yourself up too badly over this, though; it happens to the best of us.

Honey, I get it. You're pissed off at yourself for not holding out and keeping control of your online footprint. For a lot of reasons, these matters are of great importance to us all. Right now, you're probably thinking, "How could I be so stupid to not know how to set up my own privacy settings?" Well, I've got some good news to share that might just cheer you up. You see, if you add someone online and they end up being a lowlife snoop who peeps at all your posts and screenshots your salacious bikini pics, just unfriend them. Simple as that. I mean, let's be honest here; you don't need any more drama in your life than what you already get served to you on a daily basis. Am I right, or am I right?

Hell, I'll give you one better. Don't just unfriend the bastards; block them! Wipe their shitty posts and crappy selfies right off your timeline, never to be seen again. Obviously, you might face some real-life backlash for such a ruthless power move, but hey—you do you, girl.

If it ain't good for you, then it ain't good for them.

Chapter 27
IDIOTS

If there's one unflattering fact I can openly admit about myself—besides my remarkably short temper—it would have to be my lack of patience for mindless fools, pain-in-the-ass idiots, and total dipshit morons. In my many years of fabulously graceful existence, I have learned that no matter where you live or what your yearly income is, we are all surrounded by idiots. Like a stubborn fungus that grows in warm, damp places, or those fugly Croc shoes that look like Swiss cheese, idiots are here, there and everywhere.

And boy, are most of them super fucking dumb.

To put this in more polite terms—in case one of *them* might try and read this—idiots are the everyday people in your life that are so dense that every single thing they do is blatantly ass-backward, to the point that you can't help but face-palm yourself every time you're in their company. Sometimes, I wonder if society as a whole is just an elaborate stage act, like these people are part of a gigantic improv group and every character has their head shoved up their own ass. To demonstrate to you that this growing pandemic of stupidity is very real and very, very dumb, here is a short list of recent examples of the dimwits that I have encountered. But, instead of telling it in my usual bitchy fashion, I want to try a different approach. In the stories to come, I will be placing you—yes, *you*—in the shoes of the tragic simpleton in question. This is not to ridicule or embarrass you, but to give you precious insight into the walking virus that is the modern-day dumbass.

With all that said, I hope you enjoy.

VIVIENNE VUITTON

1. Unannounced, you show up at a catered dinner party that I am holding at my very swanky house. Not only are you not on the guest list and underdressed for the occasion, but you proceed to spend the entire night drinking up all my expensive, vintage booze, eating my catered food, and pestering my good friends with fart jokes and bad impressions. For anyone who has never attended a fancy get-together before, you know that you should always offer to remove the used dishes from the table when you're done eating—it's just common courtesy. As the host, it is not my duty to wait on you hand and foot the whole night. And to be quite frank, I would rather have a double root canal with no painkillers or anesthesia than spend another second watching you choke down a whole tray of coconut shrimp like an overweight pelican. And just when I think that it can't get any worse, that you can't possibly stoop any lower than you have, you decide that it would be a good idea to start insulting me in front of my friends in an attempt to get a few cheap laughs. Nice. Very well done.

    Now, if you don't mind...please get the hell outta my house. NOW!

2. You are yet another stuck-up boss with an inferiority complex—both inconsistently paranoid and tragically insecure. All day every day, you bark pointless orders at me and my terrified colleagues. This overbearing gesture perfectly expresses your desperate need to micromanage any and all issues within the office. As a raging asshole and egomaniac, you go out of your way to insert yourself into conversations that are way beyond your scope of practice (e.g., taxation issues for an expat in China or employment laws and regulations in a country that you have never even heard of). During the weekly teleconference, you do nothing but loudly state the obvious and passionately inject unformulated opinions that have little to

no relevance to the current conversation. The rest of us have no choice but to remain silent until you're done making a fool of yourself. Doubling down, you go on to adamantly support and reward incompetent employees that do practically nothing beyond kissing your ass and stroking your already oversized ego. You knowingly undermine every supervisor's authority, treating the delicate balance of power like a childhood game of marbles. Giving answers that are diametrically opposed to what others have already handed down, you have the audacity to tell your peers that they need to manage their underlings more competently. Finally reaching my limit with this disrespectful behaviour, I personally hand in my resignation letter to you. Dazed and confused by the sudden news of my departure, you scratch your big empty head and ask, "What's wrong? Aren't you happy here?"

To that ignorant statement, I have no words—only a single middle finger to raise.

3. You are my significant other and we are in a supposedly committed relationship. However, you decide that it would be a good idea to cheat on me with my best friend behind my back. I find out within a couple of days and immediately confront you. Full of yourself, you deny the allegations, even though I already went through your phone and found lewd pictures and video taken of the filthy act. Now, think about that for a brief moment. Even though you're literally on video doing the nasty with one of my besties, you still can't bring yourself to show a little bit of humility and just admit your wrongdoings. You won't, but you really should.

All right, that's enough of that. I think you get my point. Just for shits and giggles, I'll finish the rest of this section by listing a few unlabelled people that really grind my gears. These fall into the same category as common idiots, but are a lot less specific in nature. But even with broad strokes, I think you'll recognize more than a few of these social degenerates.

a) People who park in handicap spots at the mall so they can get to all the deals first. These lowlives knowingly displace the physically disabled for their own selfish needs. What kind of soulless human can do this and actually go to sleep at night, knowing they displaced some poor person who actually needed that spot? Seriously, this is utterly disgusting behaviour and should never be exhibited by anyone with a working heart and brain. For shame.

b) Guys who try to pick up women while waiting in traffic. Listen, I'm flattered that you're interested in me, but I'm on my way to work and don't have time to play Romeo and Juliet while sitting in a five-lane traffic jam. Do what most normal people do and go to a club if you want to hoot and holler at women like a drunken coyote. Hey, if you do that, then you might actually find someone who won't laugh at you and drive away like I did. No promises, though.

c) People who can't tell the difference between real Vuitton leather and the cheap synthetic knockoffs sold on the black market. Know your place and stay out of the game if you can't tell the difference. You're making those of us who actually know look bad. Just...just stop it. Okay? It's embarrassing.

d) Guys who can't take no for an answer. I know I might not be dating anyone at the moment, but no matter how irresistible you may think you are, I'm just not interested. Now, I don't want to go out for drinks or dinner with you, or have filthy, guiltless sex. I gotta...wash my hair. Yeah, that works. Listen, no means no; it's as simple as that. Get a clue and step off. Thanks!

e) Nosey neighbours who call Child Protective Services on local families for little to no reason. Unless you have kids, you have no idea what it's like dealing with young children. At their best, they are selfish, messy and disrespectful little runts who are always running, screaming, and falling onto sharp things. News flash, idiot-neighbour-who-can't-mind-their-own-business: kids accidentally hurt themselves all the time! It's no one's fault. It's just a consequence of growing up, I guess. So, just because you saw a few bruises and a scraped knee while peeping out your kitchen window at the neighbourhood children, that doesn't constitute a claim for child neglect. If you ever had kids, you sorry old fart, you might know that.

f) People who don't know how to use spellcheck. I mean...WHY?! It's right there! Just right-click the damn word and fix it! You can't seriously be that lazy, can you?! What's that? You *are* that lazy? Sorry, my mistake. Carry on, then.

g) On a similar note, people who try and use big, complex words in everyday speech. I'm very happy that you managed to read and memorize the entire dictionary by heart, but seriously, enough is enough. No one talks like that, even those with degrees and bonafide credentials to back up such flagrant douchebaggery. I get that you want to appear much smarter than you actually are, but we are all so sick of hearing you cram in these outdated phrases and words like this is a Victorian manor in 1882. It's okay to use conjunctions. No one will think less of you. Trust me.

h) Exes who can't let go. When I told you that our relationship was over, I honestly meant it and promptly moved on—as you should have done in kind. I know we had our fun (well...I know at least you had fun), but it's time to stop this weird obsession you have with me. I find it utterly bizarre and more than a little unsettling that you are cyberstalking me through my friends on Facebook, Instagram or Snapchat. I shouldn't have to say this, but this is not a good look for anyone. Just so that you are totally aware, I don't consider any of this behaviour to be darkly romantic or charming—just plain old psychotic. This crazy delusion you have about me swooning back into your arms is just that: a delusion. Pure, unaltered fiction. Do yourself a favour and just fuck off already; I'm sure there's someone out there that's just as needy and annoying as you are. Maybe they will take an interest in your trivial mind games.

i) People who can't mind their own goddamn business. I know it's intensely difficult for you to understand this, but not everything has to do with you. If you overhear a conversation by mistake, just keep on moving. Nothing to see here. It's not polite to eavesdrop. Didn't your mother ever tell you that? Please, just keep my name out of your mouth and go about your own business. If you have any, that is.

j) Assholes who drive jacked-up pickup trucks with oversized mufflers. To the inbred morons that trade their monthly food stamps for giant suspension springs and dangly truck nuts to soup up a perfectly fine truck: go to hell. You are the scum of the highway, always screeching your tires and revving your customized engine just to get the attention of strangers. Yeah, we all know you have a small and inferior pecker, no need to announce it any time there's more than one car sitting patiently at a stoplight. Just because I drive a modest, efficient Ford Focus doesn't give you the right to flex on me. Coward.

As illustrated in these numerous examples (and trust me, there are many more where that came from), it's rather apparent that we live in an ironic existence. At any given time or place, there are idiots roaming the streets in unprecedented numbers, multiplying and growing like bacteria. Please ensure that you do not slip into one of these categories and become an idiot yourself.

Once that happens, there may be no turning back.

Chapter 28
TRAILER PARK TRASH

Up until very recently, I never really understood what trailer park trash really was. It wasn't until I happened to watch an episode of the hilarious Canadian mockumentary show *The Trailer Park Boys* that I truly understood what the phrase meant. Upon first viewing the incredibly lewd show, I laughed so hard that I nearly peed myself. The random and often misguided experiences of the show's main protagonists (kind of?)—Ricky, Bubbles and Julian—came as quite a culture shock to me. I don't know about you, but I didn't grow up that way.

Because of this cultural divide, I at first thought the show to be incredibly far-fetched, although side-splittingly entertaining. In my own head, I couldn't imagine that any rational person would behave in this crude fashion. Robbing liquor stores, selling weed, and pissing in milk jugs were some of the more wholesome things I saw. But after watching a little bit more of the show and really studying the characters and their motivations, I came to realize that there are variances of trailer park trash in all of us: the good, the bad, and the very, very ugly. As a helpful guide to acknowledging your inner trailer park, here are a few indicators that some of you may be able to relate to.

1. Crashing a stranger's wedding just to hit up the free bar and cruise for women. And just to fit in and be a part of the festivities, you will make a drunken speech at the reception. Of course, when you're being thrown out, you will projectile vomit all over the entire head table.
2. Sitting down to eat at a fancy restaurant and completely flabbergasted by all the extra forks and spoons that line the dinner

table, you will use a soup bowl for the bones from your buffalo chicken wings.
3. Visiting a prestigious museum, possibly the Louvre, you'll be unable to keep yourself from giggling at all the Greco-Roman statues of naked gladiators with their small peepees and non-existent testicles. Seriously, guys, grow up already.
4. You will trade rolls of two-ply toilet paper for other valuable goods. Yeah…not much else I can say about that one.
5. You leave your baby daddy to date his brother, who just accidentally got your best friend pregnant. But when he finds out that the kid isn't his, he dumps you to hook back up with her.
6. The only actual reading you do is when your most recent court summons gets served to you.

If you have taken a look at this list and think that some of these unpleasant traits may apply to you, it only confirms that within you lies an inner hint of trailer park trash. Don't worry, though; it's not terminal.

Chapter 29
WHAT THE HELL ARE YOU WEARING? GO BACK TO THE CLOSET AND CHANGE NOW!

In case you haven't gathered this already, I pride myself on keeping a fabulously fashionable appearance. Even on those dreaded "nothing-looks-right-I-feel-so-fat" days, I still try to make an honest effort to look presentable while out of the house. However, there appears to be a large number of people who just don't care about keeping up appearances.

Why? Eh, beats me.

Regardless, it never fails to capture my attention—well, disgust, really—when I'm just strolling down the sidewalk and happen upon someone who looks like a thrift store mannequin came to life and decided to go for a brisk walk around the block. My first instinct upon encountering these fashion disasters is to stop them in their tracks and write them a formal citation for operating without a license to dress accordingly.

"What the hell are you thinking?" I'd love to ask, tearing the ticket off the pad and shoving it into their grubby little hands. "You CANNOT go out in public looking like this. For Christ's sake, there are children around!" Sternly, I would then look the poor soul right in the eye and say, "Now, you need to go home and...on second thought, don't do that. Go to the Saks Fifth Avenue around the corner, buy three or four new outfits, and never put this nightmare back on."

I know that might come off as a little pretentious of me to want to say such things, and I do understand that many of us don't have unlimited budgets and the means to purchase the latest Stella McCartney, Marc Jacobs, or Prada. There are far too many designers that just aren't feasible possibilities given the average shopper's income. I'm not asking for anyone to dress in only thousand plus dollar suits and shoes; that'd just be unrealistic. But, with all that said, is colour coordinating really that hard to do with the clothes you already have? It's so damn easy; pink and red DO NOT match, and plaid and stripes DO NOT look good together no matter how hard you tell yourself that you're pulling it off.

There—was that so hard?

To add to all of this, I see random people at the grocery store, the mall, and even the movie theaters in freakin' pajamas like they just got out of a child's sleepover. It's one thing to leave your house in a hurry and forget to change into something more formal; we've all been there at some point in our busy lives. But for the love of baby Jesus and the three wise men, don't just walk around town in the same outfit you nap and eat junk food in! Have you no shame? Contrary to popular belief, I don't desire to see your red reindeer PJs—EVER! Very classy, though.

Also, equally as important, daily personal hygiene is a MUST. Come on, guys, it takes not even five minutes to brush your teeth and put your hair up in a ponytail. I know you have at least five minutes to spare every day, so don't tell me otherwise. If you're not going to do it for yourself, then please, do it for society at large.

We would all appreciate the effort. Really, we would.

And then, you have your wannabe time travelers/vintage clothing junkies. For some (not including myself), the early '80s was a magical period of time with great fashions and designs. Be that as it may, I'm here to say that enough is enough already! The era of blown-out hair and glitter makeup has been dead and over for twenty-five years now, so just let it rest. If you are taking fashion tips from Duckie in the movie *Pretty in Pink*, then you know that your sense of style can't exactly be described as current. Simple fix: just update your wardrobe and stay away from brightly coloured leggings, bleached jean jackets, and thick leather armbands. That's about the best advice you will ever hear.

Don't get me wrong; I'm not one of those skinny bitches by any stretch of the imagination. Luckily, I have booty for days and a whole lot of curves. Because of this, I consciously try to dress for my body shape. Again, I love staying current with the latest fashion trends and the like. As you know, I am a huge fan of Vogue—both in the US and Europe. But for the record, just because that cute outfit looks good on the Amazonian goddess in all the ads doesn't mean that it will look good on you, too.

I can't stress this enough, but skinny jeans ARE NOT designed for the ladies carrying a few extra pounds in the pooch (that would include me). The salesgirl at the mall might try to tell you otherwise, but your menacing muffin top is very noticeable and very distracting. Bench is cool, and so is Abercrombie and Fitch, but their products aren't designed to be worn by flabby middle-aged women with four kids and no thigh gap. It must hurt your pride to watch your teenage daughter pull off the look without even trying, but some things just aren't meant to be. Sorry, honey. Honestly, it's just sad seeing someone try to chase that last nugget of youth.

Just let it die already.

As a citizen of the earth, I feel I should have the basic right not to be forced to view any inappropriate part of your anatomy in public. This includes—but is not limited to—your lumpy ass, veiny breasts, and the...um...tired coochie-coochie. I don't feel like I'm asking for much, but a little peace of mind would be nice.

And lastly, when attending special events like work functions, galas, weddings, and funerals, please be sure to dress appropriately. This means no leggings, miniskirts, low-cut jeans, or tube tops. As a guest at one of these classy events, I shouldn't have to avoid sneaking a peek at your goods anytime you bend over for your purse.

Other than all that, have fun!

Chapter 30
TECHNOLOGY WHORES

Remember those days when a cell phone was the size of a brick and weighed just as much? Remember when CD Walkmans were the "hot new gadget," and MTV actually played music? No? Well, that's okay. I should probably shut up now.

I'm really just giving my age away at this point.

Anyway, where was I?

Oh, right. Way back in the day when I was a teenager—when dirty pay phones could be found on every street corner and wearing seat belts while driving was a personal choice—technology was much, much different than it is today. Did you know that cordless phones back then, a relatively mundane product now, were often featured on episodes of Robin Leach's *Lifestyles of the Rich and Famous*? In those days, it was considered a luxury item to most middle-income households. But now, landlines are barely even a thing anymore, let alone actual telephones that are made for phone calls. Yuck. Times are certainly different, and technology is so much more integrated into daily life than it was when I was a kid. The thing is, I don't regret growing up that way—not one bit. These new conveniences are great and all if you don't like shopping in person, but they have their downsides, too.

With extreme convenience comes extreme laziness.

༻༺

About two weeks ago, I decided that I needed to go to an after-hours walk-in clinic to see a physician. I hadn't been feeling well for some time and finally forced myself to go see someone about it. Don't worry; this was purely mental fatigue. I had been suffering some spells of extreme anxiety for the past few months, resulting in elevated stress levels and frequent mood swings. I'm normally a very patient person, but the stress I felt every time I stuck a screen in front of my face had become too much for me to handle. That landed me in a stuffy waiting room late one night, my mind fogged with irritated sadness and anxiety.

Suddenly, for no reason, I started to shoulder surf the twenty-something-year-old guy sitting next to me. From my seat on his left, I could clearly see that he was plucking away on Instagram chat. From what I gathered in my baseless snooping, he was actively talking to his friend about how he was currently at the walk-in because of some "nasty bitch" that he thought might have given him the clap. Furthermore, he went on to say that he knew she was a "gross slut," but didn't know she was *that* gross. Immediately, I had an intense desire to slap him across the face for being so rude and childish.

Hey, dummy, I annoyingly said in my head as I continued to peer over his shoulder at the screen. *There's this newfangled device called a condom. Look it up sometime. Seriously, dude, if you knew the girl was "dirty," then why did you even sleep with her in the first place? Why even take the risk just for a little piece of easy ass? Wouldn't it have made more sense for you to just keep your pecker in your pants and wait until you found a rubber?*

Then it hit me—it was all about the convenience.

I can't believe how lazy and stupid people are in this day and age. And, to punch the point home, I had patient zero sitting next to me in the waiting room. As I surveyed the sick people that surrounded me in the cramped room, I came to a very sobering conclusion. Regardless of their age, gender, shape or size, they all had one thing in common: the addiction of being connected to their false online reality. Are people so lacking in self-reliance that they can't bypass random meaningless conversations that have little or no significance to the real world that lives and breathes all around them?

Apparently not.

※

Last night I was on the phone with my girlfriend, Shelia, and she was telling me about how she really wants to get her nine-year-old daughter a cell phone. She went on to explain to me in great detail that the phone would merely be for safety purposes so that she and her husband can check on the girl's whereabouts at all times. You know, typical helicopter parenting stuff.

"It can't be one of those cheap-o cells," Sheila surely said, continuing to fret over literally nothing. "My husband and I both agree that if we are going to go through with this, the phone has to be at least a 5G iPhone or the new Samsung Galaxy. What do you think, Viv?"

Like pulling off an old Band-Aid, I took a deep breath and let my honesty rip. "Sheila, are you asking me for my real opinion, or do you just want me to reassure you that giving your still neurologically developing child a cell phone isn't a bad idea?"

As I predicted, Sheila immediately became defensive, scoffing and citing a list of highbrow reasons to back up her decision. Clearly, she only wanted someone to tell her how progressive and trusting she was for doing such a thing.

After about five minutes of having to listen to her justifications, I bluntly interjected with, "All right, calm down. Just do what you think is right; it is your kid, after all."

Relieved, Sheila sighed and responded, "Oh…okay. Thanks for the help, Viv. I knew you would understand."

I don't know if she ever got her kid a phone, and I don't really care to know. With parents like that, they'll have bigger problems soon enough.

※

As I wrote this last section, I couldn't help but laugh at how electronic items and modern gadgets have corrupted most people to the point of developing a serious technological dependency. I don't mean to laugh at these unfortunate people, but I must admit that the whole thing tickles me in a special way. I don't know. I just hope that—in the future—we realize what has been sacrificed in order for convenience.

In the end, I'm just not sure if what we gained is worth what we lost.

Conclusion

Well, here we are—the last page. You made it to the end, and for that, I applaud you. I know you must also be somewhat shocked by most—if not all—of what you just read, and I don't blame you. That just means you're an honest person with a big heart, which is nothing to be ashamed of. I mentioned at the beginning of this book that I thought this might be a smash, but I never promised it would win a Pulitzer Prize. My goal all along was just to write something that might bring a smile to someone's face during one of life's many random, scary, irritating, annoying, and potentially irrelevant situations.

To all of my readers, thank you for checking out this book and accompanying me on a sassy journey through my petty indifferences and quirky insights. Hopefully, taking a step into my world has helped you see that it's okay to bitch on occasion. It doesn't make you whiny, ungrateful or spoiled; it just means you're human.

On occasion, it's okay to use your outside voice. You're a grown-ass adult, and I'm sure you can determine when it is and isn't okay to get a little loud. Be the most fabulous YOU that you can be, and live your own label unapologetically. Don't let the haters of the world tread on you in all your splendour, and remember that hate often comes from a place of remorse, sadness or jealousy. It's their problem, not yours.

In closing, I'd like to paraphrase my girl Nicki Minaj, who said something along the lines of, "Work on being one hell of an established bitch instead of a merely simple one."

Best of wishes, fellow bitches!

—Vivienne

What does an author stand to gain by asking for reader feedback? A lot. In fact, what we can gain is so important in the publishing world, that they've coined a catchy name for it. It's called "social proof." And in this age of social media sharing, without social proof, an author may as well be invisible.

So if you've enjoyed *The Bitchographies: Random Commentaries About Life, Love, and Knockoff Christian Louboutins*, please consider giving it some visibility by reviewing it on Amazon or Goodreads. A review doesn't have to be a long critical essay, just a few words expressing your thoughts, which could help potential readers decide whether they would enjoy it, too.

www.ingramcontent.com/pod-product-compliance
Lightning Source LLC
Chambersburg PA
CBHW021426070526
44577CB00001B/73